UNYOUNG, UNCOLOURED, UNPOOR

By the same Author

INCLUDE ME OUT!

COLIN MORRIS

Unyoung, Uncoloured, Unpoor

LONDON
EPWORTH PRESS

First published 1969
Reprinted 1970

SBN 7161 0134 8

Made and printed in Great Britain by
C. Nicholls & Company Ltd.

In memory of

MY FATHER

CONTENTS

FOREWORD

Lusaka,
Zambia

The Rev. COLIN MORRIS,
President of the United Church of Zambia,
P.O. Box 326,
Chingola,
Zambia.

Dear Sir,

You will not remember me but I met you when you visited Nyadiri in 1961 to speak, a long time ago. I was then a Form 4 schoolboy. Since, I have been 'inside' twice, once during the banning of ZAPU and another time for 'behaviour likely to cause a breach of the peace'. When UDI was declared, I left Rhodesia by the 'pipe line' and went to Uganda where I spent a year at Makerere University College. I am back in Lusaka as an official of the Party.

I wish to consult you about my problem which is this. I am a Christian of a Christian family but also a nationalist. I am tired of the insults and sneers Rhodesians receive here and in East Africa that we are cowards, drunkards and chase women and why don't we go back and fight? It has not been possible for me to fight before this time. The Party would not allow it because I had other duties here which were supposed to be more important. Now there has been a change of offices and I am free to make up my mind. I want to join the Freedom Fighters but my religion worries me. Can a Christian take up guns and sticks against his fellow man? I am afraid of God and my conscience and not of white soldiers. What if innocent people – women and children – get hurt in our battles? Is there any excuse?

You have long experience in the freedom struggle and you are also a Christian leader. I would value some advice on these matters, please.

Yours sincerely,
Daniel M. N............

INTRODUCTION

Readers who found *Include Me Out!* one-sided and unfair will, I'm afraid, think this book downright wicked. I take no pride in being provocative nor do I apologize for it. But it should be noted that the sweeping generalization made in a burst of anger has a distinguished ancestry. The Old Testament is riddled with ill-temper, and not only in its narrative passages. There is a varicosed vein of it running through its prophecy and poetry as well.

God doesn't just turn a deaf ear to the scathing tongues of his hot-blooded servants, he positively eggs them on by the example he sets. Take, for instance, that viciously unjust torrent of sarcasm he directs against blameless Job. 'Where were you when I laid the foundations of the earth?' he sneers, and then goes on for two full chapters to pile on the agony. He knew perfectly well where the poor chap was during the creation of the Universe, and it is hardly Job's fault that he didn't antedate Jehovah or lend a hand at nailing together the firmament of the sky. As though it were not enough for Job to be robbed of his wealth, health and posterity, he has to put up with Divine ridicule as well.

The Prophets were addicted to the same kind of thing. Their favourite weapon was the blunderbuss, and their hearers, innocent and guilty alike, must have spent much time digging the pellets out of their hides. After all, each of those 'fat cows of Bashan' traduced by

Amos was probably somebody's mother, and a few at least must have been harmless, grey-haired old ladies. God sanctified prophetic anger; I hope he'll do as much for mine.

It isn't symptomatic of any grandeur-delusion that I call the Old Testament to my defence. I make no pretensions to writing immortal prose, fit for inclusion in some twentieth-century canon of Scripture. I just think that there are some evils so monstrous that they have to be screamed down; some societies so oblivious of the still, small voice of reason that they must be addressed through a megaphone, even if the innocent are deafened in the process. No insult intended, but a swift kick has been known to get a mule to its feet when patient pleas failed.

Both *Include Me Out!* and this book are tracts in the tradition of the mordant Dean Swift rather than that of the charitable Bishop Robinson. I haven't the Dean of St Patrick's genius for invective which turns out to be literature, but I do share his conviction that there are some subjects that one should write about with the point of the quill and not its feather. Dr Johnson said of Swift's pamphlet, *The Conduct of the Allies*, that 'its efficacy is supplied by the passions of its readers'. *Include Me Out!* generated plenty of passion, and passion, whether in defence or attack, destroys complacency. It is all to the good if some people feel moved to lay aside their knitting and use the needle's point to pick away at the scabs of reality.

There's a job to be done not only in getting people to think straight but also to feel deep, if you will pardon the grammar. A lot of contemporary theology falls down because it is trying to resuscitate dead prophecy by laundering its shroud. It has Christians scratching their heads instead of clutching their bellies. There are plenty of stimulants on the market to agitate their already fevered brains; there's room for an emetic to clear out their clogged-up systems.

A pamphlet in the strict sense – a treatise slimmer than a book on some topic of urgent interest, written from a position of passionate partisanship – is meant, like medicine of the nastier sort, to be swallowed at one gulp. It rushes on with an indecent lack of judicious qualification to some conclusion felt by the author to be irresistible. That is why Prof. E. L. Mascall's brilliant hatchet-job,* almost word by word, on *Honest to God* was wasted effort. If the professor felt *that* strongly about the book, he should have lit the fire with it. It is one thing to swat a gad-fly; quite another to tear off its wings and gouge out its eyes. The correct response from a reader to a polemical pamphlet is either to burn it or act upon it. Like a rocket, once its incandescent light dies away, there is nothing left except the stick and a few bits of cardboard, and no amount of analysis of the debris can recreate the spectacle the watchers first saw. Whether the rocket is fired to give warning of disaster or entertain children, it is always possible that the resulting shower of sparks may reveal something that was hidden, or scorch away some undergrowth. It could, of course, burn the whole place down, but the Church is well insured and over the past centuries has proved impervious to arson.

This is a book about revolution written within sight of the barricades, which doesn't make it a good book, but does explain its subjectivity and lack of balance. It is meant to be prophecy; whether true or false, time will tell. But when the reader tests its spirit 'to see whether it be of God', I would only beg that he tries to stand

*E. L. Mascall, *The Secularisation of Christianity*, Darton, 1965, Chap. 3.

where I stand, and asks himself: if I were *there*, might I not see things *that* way?

My situation is a newly independent African State, the dust barely settled from her own freedom struggle, whose thousands of miles of border are the scene of guerrilla warfare of mounting intensity. Every day, black citizens of Angola, Mozambique and Rhodesia slip back into their own countries and engage modern military units in a vicious form of running war. My concern, therefore, with the ethics of violence has been in the first place pastoral rather than theoretical. Like other ministers and priests on both sides of the border, I have had to declare an attitude not in general terms but face to face with nationalist Christians asking whether it is right to fight, and possibly kill, for freedom. The letter which forms the Preface of this book is one of many such I have received. My reply is fictitious only in the sense that it is a compilation of all the things I have said and thought about the crucial problem it raises. However frequently the dilemma is posed, one's agony of spirit does not abate at the terrible responsibility of encouraging young men to choose death, or worse, inflict it, in preference to other alternatives which face them. No doubt if we could lift the lid off many a confessional in Latin America at the moment we would see this precise drama being played out – the same courage on one side of the grille and the same anguish on the other.

My concern is not only pastoral. Reflection on this problem over a decade ago led to the conviction that I ought to throw my derisory weight into Zambia's freedom struggle. The same question posed *to* me in the larger context of Southern Africa always leaves a more personal question *with* me – believing that other Christians are justified in getting involved in an armed freedom struggle, ought I to keep out myself? There are many reasons why this is not the place or time to offer a public answer to that question.

Include Me Out! raised in some readers' minds the question why I remain in the Church at all. This book will probably add to their doubts. The answer is banal but truthful. I remain in the Church because I have nowhere else to go. I am a socialist without a Party; an Englishman who looks in vain for honour and integrity in his homeland's attitudes towards major moral issues; a citizen of Africa with no roots here; a Westerner who believes his civilization's influence on the world is almost entirely baleful. The Church seems to share the general deadness which pervades our society, with one important difference – she alone admits the possibility of resurrection. And if we want to change the world, it is certainly true that revolution is biblical faith's illegitimate child, who left home because the Church refused to acknowledge paternity. Maybe she has similar offspring locked up in her womb and will show more sense next time. Better men than I claim to sense something stirring deep within the Church. It may not be a bad thing to allow loyalty to outstrip hope occasionally. One thing is sure. If I go under, it will be in distinguished company, not least that of those leaders of my Church in Britain and Africa who have given me the security and freedom to undertake a highly unorthodox ministry. Where else could I have that freedom or such congenial companions with whom to indulge it?

*

The title of this book is based upon a phrase that caught my eye in an edition of *Newsweek* which I cannot now trace. I am grateful to the anonymous writer for sparking off a productive train of thought, and sorry that I can't acknowledge his name publicly. Having a paranoic hatred of footnotes, I have kept the number of books quoted in the text as small as possible. I am happy to acknowledge here those works to which I am chiefly indebted for ideas and snippets of information. Many of the facts given in the chapter on the *Unpoor* are owed to Ronald Segal's *The Race War*, Penguin Books, 1967; the brilliant and moving speech by Carl Oglesby, 'Let us Shape the Future!' made at the March on Washington for Peace in Vietnam on 27th November, 1965 and printed in *The Revolutionary Imperative*, ed. Austin, N.M.S.M. Nashville, U.S.A., 1966; and *The Haslemere Declaration*, published by the Haslemere Committee, London, 1968, a justly praised practical programme of political action for getting economic change in the rich nations for the benefit of mankind. *The New Radicals*, ed. Jacobs and Landau, Penguin, 1967, is a mine of information on student revolt in the U.S.A., and was a tremendous help in writing the chapter on the *Unyoung*. Frantz Fanon's classic, *The Wretched of the Earth*, Penguin, 1967, is required reading for any of the *Uncoloured* who want to know what it feels like to be colonized and discriminated against. Many other books and articles helped to shape my convictions about revolution. Working a long way from reference libraries and newspaper files makes it impossible to recapitulate them all. I hope any authors who find their ideas clothed in my words will take it as a compliment to their influence and not proof of my lack of originality.

My chief debt, however, is not to books but people, and especially those who live with revolution, both Zambian nationalists and their comrades in exile from embattled countries in Southern Africa, who have shared with me their feelings and thoughts, and occasionally their strategies as well. In particular, Dr K. D. Kaunda, President of the Republic of Zambia, and a number of his colleagues have given me over the years a practical education in the meaning of nationalism which no books could have supplied. And I am blessed with a circle of close friends whose criticism is merciless and support unfailing. I long since gave up trying to acknowledge my debt to them.

Colin Morris,
Chingola,
Zambia.

Labour Day, 1969

CHAPTER ONE

FIRST SKIRMISH

IN TRUE theologian's style, I'll give you a one-word answer to your question and then qualify it for a hundred and fifty pages, but at least I'll give you the answer first. Yes, I believe a Christian is justified in using violence to win freedom in Rhodesia; I know no other way he can get it. I fear innocent women and children will suffer, and I badly want to add 'which, God forbid', but that is a pious subterfuge, inviting the Almighty to stave off the worst consequences of a responsibly-made decision.

My life is not at risk, nor are any of the innocents who may get hurt my kinsfolk, so it is an insufferable impertinence for me to give you any advice. My feeble excuse is that advice was asked for and not offered. I believe freedom fighters are justified in using any methods short of sadistic cruelty for its own sake to overthrow the Salisbury regime. I also believe your task is a near-hopeless one. But then, what else can you do? Go back to Rhodesia and they'll gaol you for life; stay in exile and you'll drag around, a half-man; fight them and you are almost sure to die.

You are on your own. I am sure you realize this. In the Whitehall circles where the final responsibility for the Rhodesia tragedy rests, your activities are viewed with thin-lipped disapproval or awkward embarrassment. You are rocking the boat, old boy. Revolution is not the British way of doing things. And no one will thank you for pointing out that you are the loyal subject of the Queen fighting to free your homeland, and it is the Smith gang who are the traitors. Rebels these settlers may be, but they are also white gentlemen and so must be wooed by wheedling emissaries rather than smashed by righteous power. We'll teach the blighters a lesson by cutting off their whisky supplies, but fight them? Never! They sport the same regimental ties and stood shoulder to shoulder with us in the War. So, of course, did Ho Chi Minh and his guerrillas, but that doesn't stop us from backing the U.S. attempt to fry them with napalm into an acceptance of our 'We Know What's Best for the Wogs' philosophy.

So your British guardians will bear with fortitude the prospect of your bleeding to death or dancing from the end of a rope in Bulawayo Gaol whilst they make nice adjustments to the latest peace formula before despatching it, wrapped in pink ribbon, to Salisbury. Naturally Mr Ian Smith will reject it for, as any numbskull knows, he would not survive as Prime Minister for a week if he made the slightest concession on African political rights. And logic, though not morality, is on his side. Why on earth ought he to accept a settlement whose ultimate result will be the loss of political power for ever? Would Mr Wilson agree to changes in Britain's electoral arrangements that would put his party out of power for all time? Who ever willingly gives up power? Not Mr Smith. Not Mr Wilson. Not anyone. Because we know something about white settler mentality, we are sure there can be no negotiated settlement in Rhodesia. But you'll never get that across to those cultured amateurs in Whitehall who, with serpentine cunning, knock together yet another combination of meaningless words designed to save face all round and restore God Save the Queen to the top of the pops on Rhodesia Radio.

What realism there is in the whole barmy business will be discovered in Mr Smith's Cabinet Room or those seedy Lusaka offices where black Rhodesians make desperate plans, but never in Whitehall with its pathetic faith in sanctions that may bite but cannot mortally wound. Any true-blooded white Rhodesian is prepared to weather a period of economic hardship if he thinks, rightly or wrongly, that the alternative is to lose everything he's worked for to the black hordes. And he's not without consolation. The international memory is notoriously short. Big business is always prepared to risk U.N. disapproval if there's a quick buck to be made under the Panamanian flag. Weren't we once, for about five minutes in the 1930's, going to drive Mussolini to his knees by sanctions following the rape of Abyssinia?

You are on your own because there is no longer a Rhodesia Problem as such; just an infinitely more depressing White Africa Problem. Rebel Rhodesia cannot now be smashed in isolation from South Africa, and we know how keen the West is to do something about that one! Britain may make tut-tutting noises in the U.N., but only a feather-brained idealist could see her sacrificing a thousand million pounds-worth of South African investment to moral principle. So Mr Vorster's Government will wisely ignore Britain's clenched fist in the General Assembly and take its cue from her begging hand outstretched for more trade in Pretoria.

If you look to Uncle Sam for Salvation, forget it! America finds in South Africa's rabid anti-communism a supreme virtue which overrides all distaste for her racial policies. The U.S. knows she cannot rely on the blind allegiance of any black government that might emerge in South Africa, so having made common cause with such democratic luminaries as Syngman Ree, Chang Kai Shek, Marshal Ky and Franco, she will have little difficulty in swallowing whatever Mr Vorster hands out.

Nor is there any hope of serious military intervention by the free states of Africa. The highly efficient Rhodesian and South African forces could comfortably polish off any combination of African armies during a sunny afternoon. That's not a sneer; it's a tribute to the good sense of newly independent nations in refusing to spend their meagre substance on the ironmongery of modern war whilst their people starve.

I suppose there's always China and Russia. But when they move in with an army, they are like the mother-in-law who came for the weekend and stayed ten years. And any African State that invites in the Reds courts the danger of having the United States descend with B52 bombers to liberate its population Vietnamese-style.

That leaves the United Nations, which deserves honour for its determination to construct the first fragile system of international morality. Unfortunately performance is nowhere near as impressive as protestation. There still lives in the memory the visit to Lusaka of the twenty-four valiant men of the U.N. who were going to reclaim South West Africa from the Republic of South Africa. After turning the air blue with their martial oratory, they fled back to New York post-haste when the South Africans threatened to impound their aircraft. This must be the only liberation expedition in history which failed because the liberators were unable to hire suitable transport to convey them to their destination. After that little episode, South Africans are unlikely to shiver in their beds at the thought of the righteous wrath of the U.N.

So you are on your own. And your task is much tougher than that which faced some of the African nationalists from the North who are egging you on with reminiscences of their own triumphs. In the British Colonial Power, they fought a reluctant tyrant who met them with the full rigour of unloaded fire-arms, tear gas, and with the ultimate sanction of six months' imprisonment without the option. Your South African enemies are brave and determined men from a tough stock who have defended their land by the power of the rifle for a hundred and fifty years. They won't run, because they have nowhere to run to, and their fanaticism is a match for your own.

You will take a terrible beating, and most of your own people will stand by and watch, if they are not otherwise engaged reporting your whereabouts to the police. Revolutionaries always underestimate the patience of a people under tyranny, especially if the tyrants are smart enough to give them some measure of economic advancement. Then they have more to lose than gain from the chaos which always accompanies any violent shift of power. Watchwords like Freedom and Democracy sound hollow in comparison with the healthy ring of the cash register and the good, solid slam of the door of one's own car.

Yet if you are one of those men ready, in Dag Hammarskjold's words, to gather all into one simple sacrifice, your foolhardly exploits at the Zambezi may serve to jog the memory of those men in the world's centres of power who desire to forget that you and your kind exist. Your faint cry from the Valley could keep a Prime Minister tossing in the night, whispering to him in the deep counsels of his sleep that you are doing Britain's bleeding for her, and every violent death is a charge to her account.

The Christian as Assassin

It is not too painful to fight to the last drop of someone else's blood, so the question you ask is capable of some sort of answer. The problem you pose the Church by asking it is more troublesome. We Christians make tolerably good martyrs, but are unbelievably callow when it comes to thrusting the dagger at the tyrant's heart. Possibly our reluctance is a virtue. We weep with pride in the story of Dietrich Bonhoeffer's triumphant death at the hands of the Flossenberg hangman, and pore over his last writings with an eagerness that could not be greater had he handed them out personally to us from the other side of the Beyond. But we scurry quickly away from the tougher truth that he was a justly condemned accessory to murder. Hitler, the main target of the plot, indeed survived Stauffenberg's bomb, but others in that map room were destroyed, some of them honourable soldiers. If only Bonhoeffer had lived, we lament, to tell us more about the line of thought sketched out in the startling epigrams of *Letters and Papers from Prison*. I, for one, believe that his explanation of the theology behind the bomb plot might have more to say to our time. The new theology for which the Church is searching may be hidden in that violent deed of Bonhoeffer's which misfired and not in his musings about God without religion. Any Christian, tasting the sulphur which hangs in the air of our time, could wish for a theology of violence from the pen of a great theologian who dared to strike and paid for his temerity with his life.

It is not to be. Bonhoeffer's voice is silent, and we must draw what moral we can from the story of the bomb plot. We may conclude that good theologians make bad assassins, or that the Lutheran pietism of the 1930s was a poor springboard for bold action. We do know that many of those implicated in the plot to kill Hitler were Christian gentlemen. Their last words and poise in the presence of death leave no room for doubt about that. But we can conjecture that the grisly job might have been more efficiently done by those who were neither Christians nor gentlemen. If so, what makes the Christian a poor plotter? It is a vital question. There is much smashing down as well as building up to be done in our generation, and lack of a stomach for wielding the sledge-hammer could consign Christians to the spectators' enclosure whilst Marxists, anarchists, and Black Power advocates do the brutal work necessary to break a way into the future.

A deeper question still is posed by the timing of the abortive plot to kill Hitler. Until evil is in full flower and so brazenly obnoxious that a ten-year-old blenches at the sight, Christians cannot bring themselves to use violence to destroy it. Yet the same blow struck whilst that evil is still a furtive thing of the back streets would benefit mankind more. Bonhoeffer, Stauffenberg, and the rest indeed died to rid the world of a fount of evil. Yet if they had struck ten years earlier, before the smoke of the gas chambers had blackened the sky and Europe's cities were aflame, who knows how history might have been changed? This is the cheap wisdom of hindsight, of course, worth only contemptuous dismissal. But there is a grievous dilemma here for the Christian. In 1934, Hitler, far from being castigated as a loathsome tyrant, was widely acclaimed both within Germany and outside as a dynamic, enlightened ruler carving a great nation out of the rubble of the First World War. To have killed him at that time would have reserved for Bonhoeffer a place alongside Lee Harvey Oswald instead of a position of honour in the noble army of martyrs.

If the Christian can only be sure that he is right to use violence when evil screams its true nature to the world, he will invariably strike too late. If, on the other hand, he cuts down the poisonous bloom whilst it is still a weak shoot, how can he or anyone else be sure that he has plucked weed and not wheat? And once open your mind to the need for drastic action early rather than late and you are already way out on marshy ground. Maybe the white racist who put a bullet through Martin Luther King's head might argue that he was ridding the world, or at least white society, of an evil before it achieved the zenith of its power. He could plead that he was defending his family and property by a long-range precautionary measure before things got out of his control. *We* would protest that any comparison between Hitler and Martin Luther King is so insulting as to verge on blasphemy, but that is our opinion. Who is to adjudicate? That decision carries with it a horrible burden of responsibility, and it is understandable that we should hold off making it until the last possible moment.

The reason for the Christian's hesitancy in moving to cut down evil is easy to pin-point. We have been schooled by a thousand sermons to think religiously rather than in political terms. Only when we are confronted by something that closely resembles the biblical cartoon of Satan can we screw ourselves up to draw the dagger. Sometimes those more astute in reading the signs of the times have a surer instinct for the catastrophe that looms ahead. Hence, the worldly-wise German socialists and communists were plotting violence against Hitler whilst Christians still hoped by the power of their own suffering to alter the juggernaut's course. We tried to redeem what less spiritual mortals were sure must be destroyed. In the event, neither was successful. But the episode prompts the melancholy conclusion that only a hair's breadth separates unworldly nobility from downright foolishness.

This is not a digression. It is your precise problem in asking the Church's blessing upon what you propose to do. Most Church leaders still believe that there can be a negotiated solution to the Rhodesian rebellion. They will go on thinking this to the bitter end because the alternative is too unpleasant to contemplate. They might call you a martyr if you took up arms at some time in the future, should a tolerably harsh regime become demonic. They will condemn you now as a terrorist for getting in your blow before the gas chambers are built.

Western Christians are hopeless romantics about revolution. 'The Revolution of our Time' is a required theme at most contemporary Church conferences, but if you were to eavesdrop on the discussion you would probably feel like the mourner who thought he had attended the wrong funeral after hearing the parson's tribute to the deceased. What they talk about and what you intend to do bear little relation. Revolution is ecclesiastical shorthand for the modest truth that things are changing and the Church had better change with them. Your kind of revolution, marked not by high flown talk but artistry in the use of petrol bomb and knife-thrust, is another thing again.

Take, for instance, that famous resolution passed by the British Council of Churches a while ago declaring that in the last resort Britain would be justified in using force against Rhodesia. I think they were right to pass it, but how many really knew what they were proposing? Possibly they had in mind a battalion of the Grenadier Guards crossing the border at Chirundu and engaging the Rhodesia Rifles in a good clean fight with a truce to remove casualties between each exchange of shots. How many would still have supported the resolution had it been spelled out that force in Rhodesia can only mean a messy guerrilla warfare which in order to be effective must include a high degree of terrorism – throwing petrol bombs through farmhouse windows, the ambushing of civilian cars, night-strikes against isolated homesteads? Is that what the Archbishop of Canterbury and other Church dignitaries had in mind? If so, their tough-mindedness was remarkable. Force in Rhodesia equals racial war. Military intervention by Britain or any other power could now only follow an internal struggle which reached the proportions of a civil war. That's what Mr Wilson said, and he was right.

There's an antiseptic quality about Christian revolutionary talk which robs it of realism. According to the 1966 World Council of Churches' Conference on Church and Society, 'Christians must be fully involved in the revolutions of our time'. All revolutions? Or just the good ones, the non-violent ones, or the ones where someone else does the shooting and we intone over the dead? Certainly, we are beginning to make cult-heroes of some deadly-serious Christian revolutionaries, those Latin American guerrilla priests such as the Colombian, Camillo Torres, killed in a skirmish with the police. This is partly because distance lends enchantment to the view. Guerrilla priests striving for freedom on some other continent sound romantic even to a good bishop nodding in the Lords, but God help the first curate in the London Diocese who throws a petrol bomb through the windows of 10 Downing Street! They would, of course, haul him off for psychiatric treatment on the grounds that only a nut-case could seriously believe that Britain is a revolutionary situation. Revolutions happen somewhere else: there's a British way of getting prudent change. There certainly is, and you try using it to stop the shipment of arms to Nigeria, or the employment of overseas aid as a method of putting the half-nelson on under-developed countries, or the abandonment of a hand-washing servility towards America that makes us accessories to mass murder in Vietnam! You try changing those things or any other things that bolster Britain's self-interest and you'll end up in a quarry rummaging around for a dozen sticks of dynamite let alone a petrol bomb.

A revolutionary situation is one which contains a single revolutionary. Britain numbers more than that, some of them in the Church, but certainly not as many as fiery radical preachers would have us believe. The local parish church or Methodist chapel is not bulging at the seams with revolutionaries, panting for the signal to tear down with their bare hands the ramshackle, money-grubbing structure that is all we have left of what used to be called the British Way of Life. We are prepared to lend a hand in changing things if it can all be done *nicely*. If it cannot be done nicely we are prepared to wait until it can, for we measure time by the weathering of the stone-work of our ancient cathedrals and not by the tramp of bare feet drawing closer. So we'll cheer on the guerrilla priests of Latin America and pray God no one starts up a branch of the movement in our cloister.

Fidel Castro has said that it is the duty of the revolutionary to make revolution. As the hippies would say, we Christians prefer to make love rather than war, though some doubt we have the strength to do either. We are no more cowardly than the rest, and our distaste for violence is shared by all sensible men. Often we cannot bring ourselves to storm the barricades not because we are afraid but because we are busy worshipping the sacred cow of non-violence, about which I shall have to say more later. Passive resistance has become the standard tactic of the militant Christian when confronting force. Courageous things are done under this banner by people who prefer to absorb suffering themselves rather than inflict it upon others. Possibly they are right, but as Archibald Macleish says, there are only two kinds of people in this world, the Pure and the Responsible. In many of the conflicts that give rise to revolution, our only choice is between being purely irrelevant or responsibly compromised. The flaw in passive resistance as an alternative to storming the barricades is the assumption that it is possible to foment revolutions in which we are the only ones who get hurt.

I'm afraid there's little really gritty Christian thinking on revolution to guide you. You'll have to turn to the Marxists for that. In the interests of keeping a whole skin, you would do well to study the writings of Ho Chi Minh, Che Guevara and Regis Debray. There *are* World Council of Churches documents on revolution which discuss Biblical Messianism, the Dynamics of Revolutionary Process and the Augustinian View of Social Change (I am quoting from the sub-headings of one) but don't tell you to keep your feet dry, your rifle clean, when to fight and when to run like hell. So they are of limited value.

The days of the Christian earth-shakers seem, alas, to be over – men as colourful as their names – Boglomili, the Mad Priest of Kent, Lambert the Stammerer, and Hans the Piper. They got short shift from the Church of their time; they would fare little better in a modern Church which employs gentleman-thugs to keep what the *Church Times* called 'trouble-makers' out of the Lambeth Bishops' Conference and raises not a squeak when young people are gaoled for exercising their nonconformist conscience about Vietnam by disturbing a Nonconformist Service. Here and there you might hear the faint echo of a Thomas Muntzer crying, 'The world will suffer a big jolt and the down-trodden shall arise!' But there's no shortage, too, of modern Luthers, their rabble-rousing days behind them and now in good favour with the princes, who will pronounce such men 'instruments of Satan' before donning their frock coats to take tea at Buckingham Palace.

Up-People

White Rhodesians are not your real enemy or, more correctly, they are only a tiny part of it. Behind them, back at base, are ranked the regiments that rule the world – the *Unyoung*, *Uncoloured*, and *Unpoor*. They are the Enemy, the Up-People, a triumvirate who bar your way to the future. They are the ones who poison your wells and sell you water, give you freedom and turn the key again whilst you are still celebrating. They ride on your back and shove crusts of bread in your mouth to give you strength to carry them. They are everywhere. They number not only capitalist tycoons in glass and steel towers, but also old communist campaigners growing corpulent in the Kremlin; not only cigar-chewing Texans whose wealth multiplies every time they draw breath, but also twenty-quid a week London dockers striking to preserve the purity of British blood mongrelized centuries before; not only fray-cuffed fascist parsons who use the Bible to bolster their phoney racial theories, but also celibate old men in Rome who put into God's mouth macabre words about marriage to ensure an endless supply of scrawny kids for the glory of Holy Mother Church.

As the Prayer Book never said, they are all the same

sort and condition of men – white, well-nourished, and vastly experienced. To protect their interests, wars are engineered, dictators made and broken, governments bought and sold, currencies adjusted and markets rigged. They preside over a vast Aladdin's cave into which a ragged world brings its treasure and where fewer and fewer get more and more. They are unbeatable because they make the rules. Even your cry of outrage is rendered meaningless because they own the very language you use. As they leave your mouth, your words are twisted and remoulded so that your abuse rings out like a hallelujah to their benevolence. Freedom is what *they* mean by freedom, democracy is what *they* mean by democracy, and they have the power to make *their* definitions stick. Pour forth your blazing revolutionary writings and they will oblige you by printing, publishing, and serializing them in their glossy Sunday newspapers. Then they'll bank the profits and laugh all the way home to Hampstead.

The Up-People are never down. Even war is little more than a device for redistributing wealth – amongst themselves. They made sure that Malayan rubber plantations were handed over intact to the Japanese in 1941 and that certain German tank factories (which could quickly be reconverted to producing their motor cars when the war was over) went unbombed in 1944. They talk about the value of human life, but they really believe in the sanctity of property. Hence one man gets a ten-year sentence for the foul murder of a little girl whilst other men collect forty years a-piece for the Great Train Robbery.

These are the people you have to defeat, and for allies you can count only on the rabble of Chicago ghettos and Left Bank discotheques, the scourings of university campuses, the sinister guerrillas of Asia and

Latin America, and the tired veterans of Trafalgar Square rallies. Up-People strongly approve of your non-violence campaigns because it is their windows that might get broken and their warehouses fired. But note: they are not committed to non-violence. Sing your freedom songs, wave your placards, and see that your followers sit down in orderly fashion and they will smile thinly, press the buzzer, and their lackeys will move in with rubber hose, riot guns, and dogs. And your struggles will be watched on a thousand T.V. screens with vacant incuriosity by peanut-munching helots too dim to realize that you are fighting for them, and too comfortable to care.

Up-People are bright people, powered by the pile-driving force of unbridled intellect. They are shrewd, subtle, and flexible. They know more than you. They can work the machine. They have studied you minutely and can predict your response to any situation as accurately as they sense the drift of the stock market. Youthful indignation doesn't worry them. They know the young will change their tune when they've put down the first deposit on a bungalow and have two kids in tow. The rioting poor don't faze them. If a few of those who shout loudest are bought off with a little plot of land each and a couple of pesetas in the bank they'll blossom as good capitalists. Up-People are rarely wrong.

Unyoung, *Uncoloured*, and *Unpoor* is a somewhat crude and inexact description of the Enemy. Not all coloureds are poor, just as some whites are not rich. Some of the *Unyoung* are not reactionary, and all the young are not rebels. One has to take account of plump Harlem negroes all a-gleam with gold teeth and diamond studs as well as white Appalachian share croppers who survive, ghost-like, on four dollars a day. There are African cabinet ministers, coal-black in hue, who have slipped effortlessly into the shoes and ways of their former colonial masters. And it is not unknown for bright young men with an eye for the main chance to acquire the politics and appetities of the *Unyoung* as a precaution against the day when some executive heart-beat falters, leaving a gap they can snugly fill. But these are anomalies; the average contents of the bottle conform pretty closely to the label.

So as an identi-kit picture of the citizens of a world from which you are excluded – a cartoon, if you like, over-simplified and distorted by resentment, *Unyoung*, *Uncoloured*, and *Unpoor* portrays a kind of truth. The envy of those on the outside looking in always blinds them to a few fine details, just as a slum kid sees a blurred impression of the interior of a gracious home because his nose is pressing too hard against the glass. He may get the number of chairs or the colour of the carpet wrong but the basic idea is crystal-clear – it's warm, comfortable, and well-lit in there, and damn cold where he's standing.

The first rule of war is to know your enemy. It is not enough to curse him, you must take his measure if you hope to wear him down, and that's what you will have to do, make no mistake about it. Chatty talks around the table will get you nowhere. Nothing short of cutting off his fingers will prise his hands loose from your wind-pipe. The *Unyoung*, *Uncoloured*, and *Unpoor* are Siamese triplets, served by the same blood supply and digestive system, but they must be taken apart for the purposes of dissection.

CHAPTER TWO

A CLOSER LOOK AT THE ENEMY – THE UNYOUNG

THE *Unyoung* are Establishment people. They operate the machines; all of them – political, industrial, social, and religious. Age is immaterial; their attitudes identify them. They sleep uneasily because a well-appointed world they have inherited and enriched is coming apart at the seams. The young are in revolt, a fact noted with fury by the *Unyoung* who pay the bills, endow the universities, and employ their products. It is not the vociferousness of the protest which shakes them – students always were noisy – but its universality. Student action is the only truly international movement of our time.

With contemptuous ease, young people are leaping the fences the *Unyoung* have erected and are joining hands with their counterparts across the world. Whilst the *Unyoung* squabble in the U.N., assemble their allies, and conduct propaganda wars, the young refuse to applaud the patriotism of their fathers or hate the prescribed enemy. They will neither fight nor love to order. They choose their causes, make nonsense of their own country's politics, and think the feuds of their elders utterly mad. For them, iron and bamboo curtains are not walls across the world but mental blockages in the minds of the *Unyoung*. So Czech students in Prague riot in support of the sons of good capitalists in New York. Japanese Zengakuren undergraduates snake-dance a proposed visit from an American President off the itinerary. White South African students transgress the strict colour lines their Government has laid down and support a black lecturer's right to be judged according to ability rather than skin pigmentation.

Shouting and rioting students have clashed with authority not only in the so-called liberal democracies, in Paris, London, Berlin, and Washington, but also in fascist Spain, hard-line Poland, and fanatical Peking. The *Unyoung*, having divided up the world in every conceivable way, now find yawning beneath their feet a split they did not contrive – one between generations. They discover an enemy not on the other side of the globe but at their own breakfast table.

'*Daddy Knows Best!*'

The issues may range from the trivial, the quality of the food in college cafeterias, to the sinister, germ warfare research at Porton Down and the Dow Chemical Company; but the cause is the same. The young don't like the way the *Unyoung* are running the world: they have no confidence in their judgement and precious little faith in their sincerity. They are dropping-out, sitting-down, or loving-in to make one simple point. There is a lie at the heart of all establishments and they are neither fooled nor intimidated by it. The lie is the *Unyoung's* assumption that they know what is best – for their juniors, for their nation, and for the world. The young are in revolt against the rule of the mandarin, the tribal elder, the *guru*, the wise old man replete with experience who lays down the law and by unchallenged convention sits in the driver's seat. They will not accept the establishment creed, first foisted upon them in the nursery – 'Daddy knows best!' Daddy may know more things but they are the wrong things, or possibly, he knows more things about the wrong world. The young don't see the point of the endless escalator where the eminent elder gets off at the top clutching his presentation gold watch, to allow everyone else to ascend one step nearer the cemetery.

Of course, the young's picture of the world is viciously unfair, but is it also untrue? Do not the *Unyoung* measure Ages – units of sameness – in centuries, or at least life-times, whilst the young are conscious of a world renewing itself every decade or so, rendering the life-style of one decade outmoded in the next? A parody of United States history neatly makes the point. In the 1920s the United States discovered her own rumbustuous nature, in the 1930s she discovered the world, in the 1940s fought for it, in the 1950s led it and now, in the 1960s, is paying the bill. Each decade produced its own brand of politics, literature, and folk heroes. And the hard-liners of the 1940s who erected a *cordon sanitaire* around the world to contain the Red Peril seem antedeluvian in the 1960s world of many-centred Marxism.

As the young see it, the failure of the *Unyoung* to sense the speed of change makes them prone to go ponderously on repeating the same old mistakes. Their standard response to any crisis is 'more of the same'. And it is large doses of 'the mixture as before' which wiped successive generations of young men off the globe. The survivors of the Somme and Verdun live to breed the shell-fodder of the Western Desert and the Normandy beach-heads. The French stagger out of Vietnam in 1954 and the Americans march in to repeat the same fiasco. The greedy men of the Kremlin who provoked the Cold War over Czechoslovakia in 1948 move back into Prague twenty years later to put the clock back and pour costly experience down the drain. To coin someone else's phrase, it is the bland leading the bland into every ditch in sight.

No nation is immune from the disease, not even the history-sodden British. The old fashioned imperialism that drove her out of Africa and Asia is resurrected, dusted off, and tried out again at Suez in 1956. Hence that famous headline in the *Daily Sketch* the morning Eden began his disastrous foray against Nasser – 'It's GREAT Britain Again!' The type was a little more subdued a few days later when the British scuttled out, but even in modern newspaper offices there survives the spirit of Omdurman, when Kitchener showed the wogs who was boss and a young war correspondent named Churchill, afterwards to become the most resplendent of the *Unyoung*, wrote for the *Morning Post*, 'The Egyptians came, they saw and ran away!' Good rousing stuff to read as you trotted through Green Park in a hansom cab, pausing to raise your topper to Buckingham Palace, but in 1956 it was the British who did the running and earned only ridicule and humiliation for their pains. Yet who can doubt that, given the chance, they would try it again? The *Unyoung* never learn. They go on prescribing, dispensing, and swilling the same mixture as before. It may kill more than it cures but at least the taste is familiar.

Current student protest is not in the same tradition as the japers of the Thirties who hung chamber pots from Oxford spires or the girls' dormitory pyjama-raiders of the Fifties. The young are deadly serious; it is the *Unyoung* who are frivolous. Here is irony indeed! Time was when the Unyoung shook their heads sadly at the irresponsibility of youth. Now it is the turn of the young to stamp their feet in fury at the lack of concern of the *Unyoung* for the great issues of poverty, war, and race. Is it not frivolous to project a billion dollars worth of scrap-iron into an empty sky from Cape Canaveral when just down the road in Colombia 250 infants die every day of malnutrition? That must surely be some kind of joke? Any other explanation is unthinkable in the light of the high morality of the *Unyoung*, enshrined in Rotary jingles, Masonic riddles, and the Magnificat chanted fervently before the Offertory. Britain spends more on a squadron of supersonic jet fighters which will be obsolete before delivery than on her entire overseas aid programme. It's all a great wheeze. The *Unyoung* are not cruel, they merely lack imagination. They are incapable of putting themselves in someone else's shoes for the simple reason that there are no shoes in the entire world half so comfortable as their own. So they insist on playing jokes upon mankind, and are hurt when no one laughs.

Nothing infuriates the *Unyoung* so much as the young's insensitivity to that supreme virtue – patriotism, blind loyalty to one's own side come hell or high water. Is it not treachery that students will stand shoulder to shoulder with their own generation across the world and against the interests of their native land? Yet the young believe that blind patriotism is the most destructive of qualities because it shields well-meaning people from the truth that the whole world is the smallest unit of survival in the nuclear age. And if you are looking for some line of demarcation between the *Unyoung* and young, the explosion of the first two atom bombs in 1945 is as good as any. Those born into the nuclear age are aware that they may be the last generation to make the experiment of living, whilst their seniors remain confident that the world will go on muddling through somehow. The obliteration of Nagasaki and Hiroshima may have ended a war but they cannot credit that those two mushroom clouds altered the very texture of life. More of the same! Bash on, play it cool, and it will be all right in the end!

The young think blind loyalty is foolish because it leads to such idiocies as the trial of Adolf Eichmann, the grey-faced little clerk whose only crime was that he did as he was told. Hundreds of thousands of Jews perished as a result, and the *Unyoung*, with superb hypocrisy, executed him. To be consistent they should have given him a decoration or elected him Citizen of the Year. For he did as he was told, and the *Unyoung* ask no more of any man. 'Daddy knows best!' was the philosophy Eichmann believed and put into practice.

Some process of biological selection has bred out of young people that ability to double-think which is essential to sanity and comfort in our world. Double-think enables one to detect moral distinctions in identical actions performed by *Us* instead of *Them*. It gives the United States the right to overthrow Latin American regimes which turn pink on the grounds that communism cannot be tolerated in her own backyard, yet expects Red China to view with equanimity American-armed puppets entrenched on the islands of Quemoy and Matsu not fifty miles from her coasts. Double-think allows one to draw the curious moral from the agony of Nigeria that the blacks are not fit to rule themselves and to forget that it was our booted and spurred ancestors who, with happy disregard for ethnic and geographical realities, drew those flaming lines on the map of Africa which cause nine-tenths of her problems. The *Unyoung* possess the ability to double-think in abundance and so believe that if *We* destroy the world it will be a regrettable accident whereas *They* would do it out of malice – and that makes a difference, if there's anyone around to note it. This incapacity of the young to appreciate such fine distinctions is, of course, a sign of their immaturity. But there's still hope. Maybe the scientists working around the world on germ warfare research may breed a mutation of the human species with a national flag tattooed indelibly on its soul.

Rejection of a Life-Style

It is not just the politics of the *Unyoung* which are under attack, but their very life-style. Affluence is meaningless to the young, even though they get the benefit of it. The most powerful generation of the *Unyoung* consists of the poor scholars of the Thirties who worked hard to get their degree or special skill and have slowly climbed the golden ladder, whose rungs are symbolized by the style of one's house and the model of one's car. For them, wealth is a protection against the return of the bad old days as well as the key to gracious living. They find it incomprehensible that their own children show so little interest in the status symbols that nourish them. Certainly, the young are defenceless before the charge that it is the hard work of the *Unyoung* in creating public and private systems of security that enables them to criticize in comfort and with minds free from financial worry. This is true, but the serious protestor, whatever taunts are directed against him, finds his effortless security an embarrassment, and is acutely uncomfortable in the gracious surroundings of his elders. He questions the values of the affluent society; he can take or leave its benefits. His own good fortune is soured because he knows that his fellow-students in the Third World face daily the agonizing choice between a square meal and a sixpenny exercise book. And on any reading of colonial history, there is a chain of cause and effect linking his affluence and the poverty of others, so he is ashamed.

The communist world has not escaped the lash of youthful anger. The fiery revolutionaries of the Twenties, natural heroes of the young, seem barely recognizable in the stodgy commissars who end their days as bourgeois as the Czarist petty clerks they ousted. So Moscow students read the poetry of protest at the statue of Mayakovsky, the great poet of a revolution which wound down and now grinds slowly backwards. The alienation of the young knows no ideological frontiers. Communist students riot because their Governments have gone back on their ideals, democratic students because their Governments haven't got any. Wherever they look, the landscape of the world of the *Unyoung* is barren. To the left are the totalitarian regimes which retain only the rusty machinery of the revolution and none of its spirit; to the right, machine-minding democracies which bruise the human soul by their lack of compassion if not their cruelty.

Even those targets of apoplectic colonels and self-made millionaires, the hippies, are a lounging, scruffy indictment of the lovelessness of the world of the *Unyoung*. It is not necessarily bone-idleness that impels them to contract out of socially acceptable ways of making a living. They plead the right to be human in a technologically over-developed yet emotionally stunted society. They do not know how it happens that the juices of the *Unyoung* steadily dry up to be replaced by a cold rationality except when turgid glands must be flogged into activity. They just know they don't want to end up like that. And however disreputable they may be, they hail from distinguished stock – those early Christian cells bursting out in unintelligible mouthings to express their joy, and nineteenth-century Methodist class meetings, crying and singing on mountain tops at dawn to celebrate their freedom.

Unlikely as it may seem, the protest of these colourful exotics is directed against the irreligion of the *Unyoung's* world. They scorn a Christianity whose curse is its tendency to over-definition, the fossilizing of truths which are essentially mystical into doctrinal statements as clear as crystal and twice as dead. They talk without blasphemy about Jesus as the first hippie whose unconstrained celebration of life withered at the hands of his fanatical stage-manager, Paul, who turned it into a compulsive ritualism. They pore over the holy books of Eastern religions searching for a God who will allow them a fantasy life and some degree of spontaneity. They experiment, somewhat gloomily, with sex and drugs and alcohol in dank cellars, trying to recover something of the freshness of life which machine-society has stolen from them. They are undoubtedly parasites, and no world organized along the lines of their lack of organization could help but spread the evils they claim to reject. But they put the question to the *Unyoung*: do you any longer know what it *feels* like to be human? Their own solutions may be hair-brained but that question hangs on the air, unanswered.

The *Unyoung* can quickly silence the student protestors and hippie drop-outs by asking them simply what they intend to put in the place of the things they reject. When the spokesmen of the young are allowed to state their case, the *Unyoung* are never disappointed at their inarticularity. 'There you are!' they crow, 'They demand the right to be heard, and when we give them the chance to speak, they have nothing to say!' As though that disposed of the matter! The fact that the young have nothing to say to their elders is the most eloquent thing about them. Revolution demands a new vocabulary, the employment of an unused wavelength. The words, symbols, and objects that are so comforting and familiar to the *Unyoung* have an alien and terrifying aspect to the young. They are afraid to speak for fear of setting in motion the old bandwagon with its beating drums and baying hounds; the familiar cacophony that sounds like a Te Deum to the *Unyoung* but the ring of doom to them.

The young have no gospel. They don't believe much in Communism, Socialism, Capitalism, or any other ism. Though accused of left-wing subversion, they have little interest in Communism, nor are they particularly afraid of it. Their scalps do not crawl at the well-rehearsed tales of Red atrocities. They retort with devastating logic, 'If Vietnam is permissible, what is forbidden?' Possibly they find a certain virtue in the ruthlessness of Mao, who, during the Great Famine of 1960, shot black marketeers trying to make a quick buck out of peasant hunger. Such draconian measures seem cleaner than the sleazy tricks of the capitalists who make fortunes out of the poverty of Africa and Asia. They shoot no one; they merely allow them the freedom to starve.

The young are crusaders. They have no policies, only causes, which enlist their energy and compassion for the moment. The *Unyoung* are acutely suspicious of all crusades, except those led by well-manicured evangelists who are allowed to locate a certain imperfection in their souls and correct it, provided no damage is done to their way of life. They have a horror of uncontrolled change. Possibly they sense a great emptiness beneath their feet and are terrified that someone will pull the rug out from under them. Passion, to be socially acceptable, must pass through the tortuous channels of the machine so as to emerge as bland as water and not half as dangerous when taken in quantity.

Choices That Make No Difference

Settle for low success and avoid the risk of high failure – that is the way to get on. The mentality of the *Unyoung* has that nice sense of balance pilloried by W. B. Yeats:

> *A levelling, rancorous, rational sort of mind,*
> *That never looked out of the eye of a saint*
> *Or a drunkard's eye . . .*

This is the mentality which dreads having to make choices that could change things and so constructs political systems where every button you press guarantees you more of the same. The British voter can take his pick between a Government which contrives to be tepidly socialist by whoring after international capitalism or an Opposition so spineless that its Parliamentary attack reminds one of the caperings of a court jester tapping a drunken king on the head with a pig's bladder. And the American elector recently had the freedom to select Humphrey or Nixon – a non-choice so exquisite as to render democracy meaningless. The important thing is that change must make no difference. That is the basis of liberal democracy – plenty of choices and a virtually total absence of different things to choose from.

No sign shall be given to this generation, said Jesus, but the sign of Jonah. No choice must be offered to this generation, declaim the *Unyoung*, except the choice between black zebras with white stripes and white zebras with black stripes. And you will earn ten bonus points and a crack at the big money prize if you can state, in not more than fifty words, why black-striped white zebras and white-striped black zebras are not the same, never have been or will be, and why any self-respecting democracy will fight to the death to preserve the precious distinction. Unfortunately, the young, like the boy in the fairy tale who announced that the king was naked whilst the intellectuals cooed over the cut of the mythical clothes, have cottoned on to the fact that our political system only offers them non-choices. But what can they do about it?

The protest of the young has an hysterical overtone because of their frustration. The key to the future seems locked away in a thief-proof safe, along with the combination. They voice their despair in folk songs:

Junk your principles,
Don't stand up and fight,
You won't get democracy
If you yell all night.

Or, as the Port Huron Statement of the Students for Democratic Society puts it, 'We are imbued with urgency, yet the message of our society is that there is no viable alternative to the present.' They are beating a great rock with a feather duster and eventually it is the duster which disintegrates. The machine is too complex and powerful for them. And more than that, the machine changes people. This is why Robert Kennedy's death caused young people greater anguish than that of his elder brother, the President. John F. Kennedy was a tarnished hero. The machine changed him, and resulted in Cuba and Vietnam. He had to come to terms with the powerful senators, the fixers and party managers. The young allow themselves the illusion that Robert Kennedy died with his ideals intact. The *Unyoung* smile at such naïvety, knowing that politics is a mélange of sordid deals and compromises. They announce that politics is a dirty game with a note of pride in their voices like the undertakers and hangmen who get a kick out of other people's abhorrence of their work.

The tougher-minded of the young people have accepted that this is the way things are, and have lost interest in formal politics. They toy, instead, with revolution as a way of changing things. They choose for heroes left-wing freedom fighters such as Ho Chi Minh, Fidel Castro, Che Guevara and Cammilo Torres, men of steel who gave up the attempt to work through the system and took up arms to smash it until not one stone was left standing upon another.

It is the *Unyoung's* refusal to be shocked by their outrageous behaviour which drives the young to ever greater extremes. The love-ins and drop-outs get more bizarre, the speeches wilder, and the threats more melodramatic. The *Unyoung* smile indulgently and preen themselves upon their tolerance. It is only when their property or social power or incomes are threatened that they get nasty. Then the joke is over and the prison vans begin to roll. Short of this, the *Unyoung* rely upon a secret weapon to take its toll – the clock. The young get older, and slowly come to terms with the machine; increasing prosperity and family responsibilities blunt the cutting edge of protest. But the clock is against the *Unyoung* as well. They die. And what will they leave behind them – more of the same?

Possibly, but there is a new element in the atmosphere. Student protest may die away, but it will leave behind it a volume of untapped social energy and unengaged idealism which in the right proportions could become explosive. The kindling is laid; this much student protest has achieved. Each one has added his twig to the pile.

It awaits the first shower of sparks which results when a big enough spanner is thrust into the machine, and then there'll be an almighty bang.

So the magnificently decadent society of the *Unyoung* will outlast this round of riots and protest. The *Unyoung* have the power. The question is: have they the patience? They cannot be beaten, but they can be worn down. Their ageing bones and hardening arteries can stand only so much tension. And the price of supremacy is tension. Ask any white South African. He is firmly on top, but around him is a growing mass of under-dogs who create a psychological pressure by their very existence. And he wonders whether in every smiling black face there is a calculating eye, measuring him up for the knife thrust; whether any minor clash will spark off the conflagration that will put a permanent end to his peace and comfort. It is the dreams of the *Unyoung* that are invaded first by formless threats and strange forebodings. The action comes later. The *Unyoung* have the wealth, the guns, and the know-how. They have everything except time. That alone belongs to those who all over the world have begun the process of attrition – the wearing down and the tiring out of the unbeatable.

My account is marred by a double distortion. It romanticizes the young and does much less than justice to their elders. But revolutionaries cannot afford to be fair in the *Unyoung's* sense of the word, the careful balancing of both sides of the case. If you choose extremism as a way of life, you will have to close your mind to qualifications, excuses, and justifications. Extremism demands a narrowing of perception until it is brought to a pin-point intensity like the sun's rays through a magnifying glass. Love only permits extremism if breaking down will clear the ground for something better. That is the gamble. You are pitting your wisdom against theirs, your understanding of Christianity, even, against their version of it. You are gambling that when the smoke finally clears, a way to the future will have been opened up. And you can only strike with determination if you are prepared to make the boldest of affirmations, that God is behind the revolution. It needs strong nerves to say it. It takes even stronger nerves to act upon the assumption, for revolutions can be cruel and destructive as well as creative and liberating. The last public words of Camillo Torres, the Catholic priest who led a guerrilla band in Colombia, were: 'After the revolution we Christians will have the peace of mind which is grounded in love of the neighbour. The struggle will be long. Let us begin today.' Six weeks later he was dead. Unless you have such stark self-confidence that some might call faith, it is better to make your peace with the *Unyoung* and settle for what they are prepared to offer you.

CHAPTER THREE

A CLOSER LOOK AT THE ENEMY – THE UNCOLOURED

GOD knows, I can't tell you anything you haven't already discovered about life in the ghetto, but there are some things you ought to know about the *Uncoloured*, or possibly that I need to set down to get them out of my system.

You will probably agree that most of the *Uncoloured* are nice people. That is half the problem. It is only when you move in next door to them or get caught with an arm round their daughter that they get really ugly. The reason is the same in both cases: you are destroying the value of their property. Those silly liberals who rant on about white South Africans as though they were all *sjambok*-swinging, bloody-fanged monsters are a mile wide of the mark, and lack a true sense of the tragic. You will have found out by now that it is, within a given context, a much kinder fate to fall into the hands of a white South African than a post-war British immigrant to Africa. Those who don't believe this should ask themselves why over a million Africans from other territories have settled in the Republic and scream with anguish when they are threatened with repatriation to their homelands.

South Africa is the scape-goat of the *Uncoloured* world because she cannot hide her sickness, or maybe she doesn't even bother to try. Anyway, that's the place where the rash comes to the surface. The rest of the world contrives for the most part to itch in private, but is equally diseased. Watching Britain's contortions recently when a few thousand Kenyan Asians begged her to discharge her solemn obligations towards them makes one tremble for what would happen if Britons, like white South Africans, were outnumbered seven to one by blacks in their own land. Sophiatown would be paradise compared to Wolverhampton, and Mr Enoch Powell would probably head a coalition Government with Sir Oswald Mosley.

If the *Uncoloured* were not in general such nice people things would have come to the boil long before this. I doubt that your people could have wrung a victory out of the resulting cataclysm but at least the battle line would be clearly drawn and the *Uncoloured* brought face to face with the terrible anger of the wretched of the earth. As it is, there are still parts of the world, especially South Africa, where the comfortable ruts of a feudal existence, well-oiled by a strange mutual tolerance, keep traffic between the races moving smoothly along predictable lines.

Provided the black South African keeps clear of politics, he has a better than even chance of a pleasant life. His children can run bare-assed in the *veld* with those of his white *baas*; he'll be nursed when sick and pampered when old. The pastoral idyll of the Afrikaans farm with the fair, tough-minded affection of the *boer* warmly encompassing black workers, dogs, and cattle alike, makes credible the claim of the Dutch Reformed Church that this is the way God intended it. It is only when the black South African probes the limits of his existence that he finds it is bounded by barbed wire. And the ominous *twang* of the parting wire is jerking the *Uncoloured* throughout the world out of their centuries-old dream.

When William E. du Bois, crack-pot visionary and founding-father of the Pan-African movement, declared in 1900, 'The problem of the twentieth century is the problem of the colour line – the relation of the darker races to the lighter', he was treated as a case of premature senility. There seemed no scrap of evidence to back his judgement. The American negro whistled merrily as he shined your shoes, Indian Princes dispatched their annual Loyal Addresses to the Great White Queen, replete with *salaams* and accompanied by chests of precious stones, and in a thousand packed meetings, missionaries assured white Christians that Africans and Asians were eagerly receiving the gospel and singing the songs of Zion in pidgin-English. A few scientists claimed to see in the future the engulfing of the world by the Yellow Peril, but their predictions were filed in the fiction section of the libraries along with books of Jules Verne and H. G. Wells. The universe turned solidly about its axis, generating wealth for the *Uncoloured* at every revolution.

Occasionally blacks stepped out of line. Then Southern American gentlemen got out their lynch ropes and branding irons, protected by a Constitution which declared judiciously that a negro was three-fifths of a man. In India, during the First World War, a General Dyer shot down four hundred of Gandhi's followers at Amritsar, and though dismissed from his post, returned in triumph to Britain to be rewarded with a gratuity of £30,000 subscribed by readers of the *Morning Post*. King Leopold of the Belgians dealt with every form of black indiscipline from theft to unpunctuality in the Congo by hacking off right hands. It was all good, clean fun, and part of the educative process of a world which, in the words of Sartre, numbered two thousand million inhabitants: five hundred million men and one thousand five hundred million natives.

For centuries the black man encroached upon the world of the *Uncoloured* only as an amusing freak – a time symbolized by the compleat gentleman whose entourage included a blackamoor in a velvet uniform bearing an ostrich-feather fan, and a dog which stood on its hind legs to order. African slaves in New Orleans markets were advertised as 'rare novelties' if they could speak a few words of English or make a courtly bow to a lady. They were almost, by some odd chance, human beings. Things change slowly. Modern negro entertainers and sportsmen such as Sammy Davis Jnr. and Cassius Clay put up for long enough with being gawped at because they could actually do something as well as the white man. Then they cottoned on to the fact that they were being used to prove some obscure racial point and turned back to their own people, seeking Black Power instead of white patronage.

It is hardly surprising that your own view of the past differs dramatically from the yarns the *Uncoloured* tell their children of the kindly white hand reaching down to pluck the black barbarian out of the pit. The American negro's story, for example, was lived out against a fiery back-drop of pain, bone-breaking labour, rape, and humiliation. There was for him no such thing as casual existence. To stroll down a street was to gamble against meeting violence before reaching its end. Life was safe only at the price of humility telegraphed ahead of him by a huge, deferential smile. To walk tall like a man was to invite a shove into the gutter. If he stepped out of line with a white woman, even through a misunderstanding, he would be castrated by white men who had told ribald stories about his supposed potency whilst they worked off their own sexual insecurity on his womenfolk. Always he had to smile – when ordered around by arrogant little white boys, or as he watched his women defamed and his old people terrorized. He had to smile because a solemn black man was an arrogant one, throwing down a challenge which was answered by a violence he dare not return.

From time immemorial, the *Uncoloured* have cast the black man in the role of a clown, and he has obliged by turning somersaults in return for a crust of bread or a discarded jacket. To get anything he had to fawn and wheedle, extolling the generosity of his masters when for a change they favoured him instead of their dogs with the debris of the dinner table. For it did not satisfy the *Uncoloured* that they had everything: it was the black man's God-ordained vocation to make them feel good about it as well. So by violating his manhood and crawling he might get an education for his child or medicine for an ailing wife. The *Uncoloured* were sparing of everything but their religion. They handed that out in large doses and rejoiced to hear negro voices singing those haunting spirituals in which a heavenly reward is promised in return for earthly obedience. They thrilled to the thunder of bare feet performing tribal dances, and never realized that they were witnessing not quaint ceremonials but training sessions. The black man was flexing his muscles against the day when he would refuse to dance to the master's tune and would use his energy instead to tear apart the Garden of Eden.

The *Uncoloured* do not recognize this version of their history because they are blind believers in their own myths. They claim to know the native, and they are right. They invented him. The 'native' is a snake's-nest of half-truths, ill-digested experiences, and wild surmises. The black man is lazy. The black man smells. The black man doesn't appreciate kindness. The black man is a thief. Some black men were lazy, smelly, unappreciative, and light-fingered, for human vices are spread fairly evenly throughout mankind. But other black men turned the myths against the myth-makers. Laziness was an early form of passive resistance, theft a kind of unorganized sabotage, and a sullen nature a psychological pressure. The *Uncoloured* congratulated themselves upon their cleverness, and boasted that no native could put one over on them as they watched the black man digging away industriously. They never noticed that he was digging the ground from under their feet to produce a grave into which the 'native' would be interred along with Father Christmas, the fairies, and other legendary creations of the human imagination. When the curtain finally came down on the colonial drama, the masks were stripped off, and the *Uncoloured* found themselves confronted by a stranger who might well have stepped out of a flying saucer from another planet for all the insight they had into his nature. The *Uncoloured* had been close to a man and hadn't seen him; touched him without feeling anything; heard noises and never detected there was someone there.

The *Uncoloured* were doubly deluded – that their myths were true and their values universal. *Their* values alone were the planks upon which a civilized life could be built, so the black man had to learn them, humbly accepting as paganism anything in his way of life which differed from theirs. Some black men, quick to sense the over-weaning vanity of the *Uncoloured*, worked hard at the business of aping their betters and won for themselves special privileges. Like lilies on a slimy pond, the black élite materialized, the odd doctor, lawyer, parson, or teacher who paid the *Uncoloured* the supreme compliment of slavish imitation. They talked in Oxford accents, wore natty suits, and bemoaned their unhappy fate that they shared the same skin colouration as the black masses. Their hearts and their future were with the *Uncoloured*, who were lost in wonder at the verisimilitude of these talking dolls. Western genius had added a new mutation to the human species – what has been called the Graeco-Roman negro, and specimens were sufficiently rare to prove that the gap between the races was, as they had always thought, almost but not quite unbridgeable.

Black élites served another purpose in the world of the *Uncoloured* besides proving that its values were for limited export. They were a cushion against the shock of racial collision. Their gentlemanly political associations made apologetic mock war upon the *Uncoloured*, rattling the pen rather than the sabre. They lobbied not to get their own people the freedom of the land, but to win for themselves entry into white clubs and masonic lodges. And it pleased the *Uncoloured* to grant them a few concessions so that their sense of justice might be applauded and their Christianity shown to be sincere.

Those Graeco-Roman negroes who did not eventually sicken of the charade and return to their own kind shrivelled in the hot winds of nationalism. They were of no further use to the *Uncoloured*, and their own people swept them contemptuously aside. They lingered on like the rusting equipment of some abandoned project. It was all very sad. The *Uncoloured* almost succeeded in evolving a type of black man who did not fight, smell, or make threatening noises; who could balance a cup and saucer on his knee and eat cake with a fork.

History Re-Written

Who was it that said history is always written by the victor? The *Uncoloured* had written all the history books because they firmly believed that history only happened to them. And in one sense they were right. If by some trick of time their great-grandfathers had returned to the twentieth-century, they would have wandered about dazed, quite without landmarks, and aghast at the marvellous things their descendants, moving through history, had done. Yet the seventeenth-century forbears of the Egyptian fellahin, Indian peasant, or Central African tribesman could return to earth today and feel perfectly at home. Nothing significant would have changed. The back-breaking labour, the struggle against hunger, the sheer pain of bare life would be little different from what they had known hundreds of years before. History *had* only happened to the *Uncoloured*, and their glowing account of their achievement rivalled the Book of Genesis as a picture of order being created out of chaos. The detail varied, but the key-motif was always the same; some *Uncoloured* missionary, explorer, or soldier set foot on strange terrain, planted a flag, and cried 'Let there be Light!' and a black man rose uncertainly on his hind legs and begged.

In the turmoil that followed the Second World War, the brittle world of the *Uncoloured* splintered, and they found it prudent to re-write the history books. Their second attempt was hardly more subtle than the first. In place of the old blanket condemnation of black savagery was substituted their anthropologists' appreciation of the glories of tribal life. White scholars seized upon a black poet's one-word celebration of his colour – *negritude* – and blew it up with intellectual hot-air into a philosophy, pouring out their learned books and papers to romanticize what they hadn't even noticed before. Missionaries pensioned off the harmonium and brought the drums into church. They suddenly discovered that practices they had struggled for a century to stamp out fitted in nicely with something called indigenous theology. They faced the startling possibility that God had been at work amongst black peoples before they arrived from Europe to announce His existence.

The *Uncoloured* still allowed themselves the odd lie, and boasted of giving freedom to half of Africa and Asia. They didn't, of course; the black man took it. He rattled the bars of his cage to such effect the whole building threatened to collapse, whereupon the *Uncoloured* beat a strategic retreat and claimed the credit for what they couldn't prevent. The process of teaching colonial peoples to read and write appeared in the new histories as education for freedom. But that was an afterthought. The blacks were taught to read and write because a plentiful supply of petty clerks was required to tick off the cargo manifests as the treasure was loaded for Europe. Literate evangelists were needed to preach that gospel of hard work and obedience which some of the *Uncoloured* found a useful adjunct to the King's African Rifles in keeping order and discipline.

When the reckoning began, the *Uncoloured* found themselves in a web of their own devizing. Having agreed privately amongst themselves that violence was the only language the native understood, they screamed outrage when he began to speak it. They had always thought the black man lazy and slow, but now his speed frightened them and they pleaded with him to be reasonable, to slow up and be patient. That was the word which went round the world. Tell the black man to be patient so that time can be bought in which to puzzle out some way of getting the lid back on the witch's cauldron. But their supply of credibility had run out. Martin Luther King wrote from an Alabama gaol:

For years now I have heard the word 'wait'. We have waited for three hundred and fifty years . . . I guess it is easy for those who have never felt the stinging darts of segregation to say 'wait'. But when you have seen vicious mobs lynch your mothers and fathers at will and drown your brothers and sisters at whim; when you have seen hate-filled policemen curse, kick, brutalize your black brother with impunity; when you see the vast majority of your twenty million Negro brothers smothering in an air-tight cage of poverty in the midst of an affluent society . . . when you are harried by day and haunted by night by the fact that you are a Negro, then you will understand why we find it difficult to wait. . . .

The Second World War destroyed many things – one of them was the myth of Black Savagery. Having for centuries told the black man how degraded and brutal his past was, the *Uncoloured* then perpetrated Belsen and Buchenwald, Nagasaki and Hiroshima. Chaka's assagais seemed the toys of children compared to the flame-thrower and napalm bomb. The *Uncoloured* recruited hundreds of thousands of black men to help them free Europe from Nazi domination, and told them they were fighting for the precious right of any people to rule themselves. The black man got the point. What was permissible to free Europe could not be forbidden in India. What was right for the French or Poles could not be wrong for Kenyans or Nigerians. Adolf Hitler gave the coloured races their freedom by exposing the contradictions at the heart of Western civilization. Teachers cannot control the uses to which the knowledge they deliberately or unconsciously communicate is put. Negro marines in Vietnam, having been trained at great expense to kill, will return to the United States replete with terrible knowledge, and God help the first white thug who tries to push them around! What they learned in South East Asia will be put to use on the streets of Chicago.

Time of Reparation

The coloured peoples have woken up to the fact that they have been used, fooled, and lied to. The black man's heart, swollen with rage, humiliation, and sorrow, has finally burst. And he is tearing at himself in fury to remove the last traces of the *Uncoloured's* touch. Those who feel deepest have even abandoned the surnames foisted on their ancestors by slave owners, and call themselves simply Malcolm X or Michael Y because no *Uncoloured* in the history of the world has ever owned such a cryptic name. They are hieroglyphics without a history for men who are about to make their own history. They are rejecting Christian names which symbolize their baptism into the world and religion of the *Uncoloured*, and are proudly flaunting the tribal names they dared not use in the missionary's presence or those adopted from a Muslim faith in whose militancy and fierce pride they rejoice. They worship Allah because he is a god who from time immemorial has received the praises of black men alone.

Those *Uncoloureds* who imagine that the black man will be content with his freedom are deceiving themselves. There is reparation to be made as well. That is something else the War taught him. The occupied countries of Europe were not content to be rid of the Nazis. They demanded, and got, compensation for their unlived lives and ransacked treasure. So the colonialist will not be able to buy his way out of the trap by the bare grant of independence – as though a piece of paper with an imposing seal on it evened up the score. What about the reparation for generations of unlived lives, the great cataract of treasure which flowed into Europe and made her great – gold, diamonds, ivory, cotton, rubber, and slaves? The *Uncoloured* are disgusted that their generous gift of freedom is received in silence. Their claim to have educated the black man is greeted by a hollow laugh. They certainly taught him: they taught him to use a shovel and make them rich; to pick cotton and make them rich; to shin up rubber trees and make them rich. The West did not make the black man. The black man made the West.

If you could reclaim your plundered treasure, the West would be as bare as a house furnished on the never-never after the bailiffs have gone. That very name, 'the West', used to denote a geographical location, then a proud achievement; now it serves to identify an undischarged bankrupt. It represents a nervous condition, a slinking avoidance of the truth as comical and humiliating as Andy Capp dodging the rent man. The *Uncoloured* resent you because you are putting an end to a luxurious life lived on tick. They still have the appetites of a man-eater, but lack the teeth.

The world of the *Uncoloured* is doomed. They are doing you a great service when they put up the immigration barriers against your entry, like the inhabitants of a pox-ridden house locking themselves in with their pestilence. The glory of the West is only a magnificent decadence hidden behind a phalanx of gleaming machines which are the last kick of the Renaissance. There is plenty of activity, but it is not the disciplined movement of men of purpose. It is the crazy gallop of a chicken with its head cut off. Just a reflex. Behind the baroque frontage – the elaborate ornamentation which spells the end of an age – is emptiness.

Everything has deserted them, inspiration, art, even God. For on the basis of their own theology, presumably a God who appears in history can also disappear. They talk about the Death of God, but it is more likely that he has withdrawn in disgust.

Because coloured immigrants pour off every ship and airliner, the *Uncoloured* like to believe that they have something precious the rest of the world covets. If they had any sense, they would see this not as a pilgrimage to Bethlehem but as the sacking of Constantinople; it is the looting of a burning store, the collection of jetsam from a foundering Leviathan. Why shouldn't the black man come to the West? There are all sorts of good things to be picked up, including an excellent education, and his forbears have already paid for them in blood.

The *Uncoloured* are beyond renewal because they cling to the pathetic idiocy that it is their divine vocation to renew everyone else. They are a frightened people who for centuries have handed it out but can't take it. Only in the most negative sense do they qualify as examples. Heed some wise words of James Baldwin:

> White people cannot, in generality, be taken as models of how to live. Rather the white man himself is in sore need of new standards which will release him from his confusion and place him once again in fruitful communion with the depth of his own being. . . .

Even your mistakes must be your own and not a parody of theirs. Like over-possessive parents, if given the chance they will try to live on through you when their time is done.

It was to be expected that the *Uncoloured* would try the old trick of staying on top by making a few concessions, such as constructing a meaningless multiracialism within a framework of giving nothing away but the time it takes to patronize you. So the old colonialists have been replaced by a new breed of functionaries who make a living out of coloured misery by becoming experts in something called race relations. And there is no shortage of charming liberals who hope to establish a respectable pedigree by adding a few unpronounceable African names to their guest-lists. They will wear your national dress, squat cross-legged on the floor reciting the poetry of Aime Caesare, and even sleep with the odd coloured girl. They are collaborators, not comrades. Multi-racialism is a fraud in any situation where one race starts with everything and the other with nothing. All you'll get is charity, not justice. Rather than waste your time chatting about *negritude* with white negroes who sleep between silken sheets, you would do well to follow Stokely Carmichael's suggestion – go home and tell your daughters they are beautiful.

The Black Power boys are right when they claim that the domination of the world by the *Uncoloured* was achieved and maintained by violence, and will only be overthrown the same way. So long as the negro is well-behaved, humble, and responsible he will be praised for being civilized and get a few crumbs – a Nobel prize for Martin Luther King, a seat on the Supreme Court for Thoroughgood Marshall, a Red Hat for the odd black bishop, and a big hand for Eartha Kitt. It is a sad fact that only when the negro starts burning the place down will the life of his rat-gnawed children get any better. That's what Michael X said, and they gave him twelve months in gaol for saying it. On the other hand, when Mr Enoch Powell delivered the diatribe which reinforced the secret racialism of a whole nation, he earned a tut-tut from the Archbishops and a disapproving leader in *The Times*. That's the only kind of justice you'll get until you lift society off its hinges.

There is now only one world, plus the West. Greed is the most divisive force on earth, and the *Uncoloured*, in tearing at each other's throats, have united the wretched of the earth. The writings of Che Guevara have been found in the knapsacks of dead Vietcong; Black Power leaders study the works of Ho Chi Minh; Fidel Castro is a hero in the slums of Manchester and Harlem. The coloured world is finding wholeness. The West, which once sailed majestically through space like a sun, drawing the other regions of the earth into her orbit, grubs along, trying frantically to co-exist with a world in revolution.

When the thought-world of the *Uncoloured* finally collapses, you will have to replace it with something more substantial than a romanticized version of the Black Past. Above all, you must learn the moral of the West's spiritual bankruptcy. It is futile to exchange a God locked up in fourth-century Greek concepts for the projection into the heavens of a primal Black Shape. You know that famous poem of Dr Armattoe:

> *Our God is black,*
> *Black of eternal blackness,*
> *With large voluptuous lips,*
> *Matted hair and liquid brown eyes,*
> *For in His image we are made.*
> *Our God is black. . . .*

That is rubbish. You may as well go back to worshipping the spirits of mountains and rivers as gaze into a mirror at your own faces and intone 'Our Father . . .'

The history of the West is a record of the attempt to

use God; to harness him to our engines and drag him like the Trojan Horse into our crusades against the enemy of the moment. Having deserted the cathedrals of the *Uncoloured*, he will not settle down happily in any black republic. The White Man's God has failed to unite mankind. There is no reason to believe a Black Man's God would do any better.

CHAPTER FOUR

A CLOSER LOOK AT THE ENEMY – THE UNPOOR

INCREASINGLY, the subject of hunger is worth little more than a polite yawn in the rich world which reacts with dead eyes to those Oxfam horror pictures showing swollen-bellied babies tugging hopelessly at their mothers' wrinkled breasts. World poverty statistics are beginning to bounce off the Up-People, whose twinges of guilt have eased into vague irritation. They have dug up all the old coal-in-the-bath sneers of Depression days to prove that if most people on earth are underfed, it's their own silly fault.

In spite of the great work being done by charitable organizations, or maybe partly because of it, the *Unpoor* have settled down to a long siege, grimly determined to hang on to what they've got, to the last drop of blood of the mugs they pay to do their fighting for them. Heart-rending propaganda will not shame them out of their near-monopoly of this world's goods. Governments don't feel shame, and it is government by the rich for the rich that guards the gap between the Haves and the Have-nots against shrinkage during our lifetime or anyone else's, short of bloody revolution.

It is greed, not love, that makes the world go round. It writes its own laws, finds work for every human vice, and demands the right to exploit any human weakness. There is an extreme but instructive example in

William Shirer's *The Rise and Fall of the Third Reich.* It is a routine business letter and runs:

> Following our verbal discussion regarding the delivery of equipment of simple construction for the burning of bodies, we are submitting plans for our perfected cremation ovens which operate with coal and which have hitherto given satisfaction. . . .

In its smooth formality, that letter has the ring of the Head Office about it – oak panelling, lush carpets, bowls of roses, and svelte secretaries. But it is talking about a shrieking hell in which mountains of grotesquely-stiffened corpses were stacked like logs of wood, where living skeletons extracted gold fillings from the skulls of dead ones, and little children were hung up on hooks, hidden in their mothers' discarded clothes in pathetic efforts to save their lives. But as they say, that's business. Wealth shapes its own ethic. The *Unpoor* believe that if there is a market for *any* commodity, it is their sacred obligation to supply it.

The *Unpoor* have turned greed into the highest form of patriotism. Anything goes, so long as it has a favourable effect upon our Balance of Payments. The British say: if we don't supply arms to Nigeria, the Russians will. Either way, thousands of poor devils will be robbed of the only thing they have left, life itself, but at least the nice rich will benefit rather than the nasty ones. And it *is* a link with the Old Country to have your child killed by a bullet made in Britain.

Because this is the way things are, those fine people who have taken on the job of persuading the rich nations to double their international aid are spitting against the wind. The occasional charitable impulses of wealthy countries stand out like gold fillings in a mouthful of decay. They will use any weapon to hand, not excluding violence, to bludgeon down a poor world struggling to the light.

Life in America's Back Yard

The wealthiest of all nations, the United States, has repeatedly brushed aside international law and trampled national frontiers to foil the attempts of wretched Latin American peasants to gather a few extra crumbs for their bleak tables.

For example: *In 1954, a democratically elected Guatamalan leader called Arbenz wanted to reclaim 400,000 acres of unused land owned by the United Fruit Company of America, so that more of his people, half of whom live below the poverty line, could feed off their own little patch. He offered the U.S. company reasonable compensation. The answer was swift and brutal. In a coup engineered by the Central Intelligence Agency, Arbenz was overthrown and replaced by a military junta dedicated to cherishing big land owners, the 2 per cent of Guatamalans who have 80 per cent of the land.

Or what is one to make of the strange goings on in the Dominican Republic, centre of the Caribbean Sugar Bowl?* When a popular uprising threatened the *status quo*, 20,000 marines were dispatched to shore up the military dictatorship and put down the peasantry. The United States' sugar interests, which had a big stake in the military junta's survival, were not unpleased. How the peasants felt is another matter. No one bothered to ask them.

Then there is Cuba, whose bitter quarrels with the

*Carl Oglesby, 'Let us shape the Future' in *The Revolutionary Imperative* ed. Austin. N.M.S.M. Nashville, 1966.

United States, though officially about politics, have really raged around markets. It all began when Fidel Castro accepted a Russian offer to supply crude oil cheaper than the Americans were doing. U.S. companies in Cuba refused to refine it, and because they had the only processing plants on the island, they were nationalized. America retaliated by cancelling Cuba's sugar quota and setting up an economic blockade. When this failed to bring Castro to heel, the C.I.A. talked a reluctant John F. Kennedy into agreeing to an armed invasion of Cuba which ended in disaster at the Bay of Pigs.

Cast an eye on Brazil, home of the coffee bean. In 1964, with U.S. naval support, President Goulart was toppled by General Ademar Barros, who received a warm telegram of congratulations from President Johnson. Unhappily, the mutual joy did not long survive. Brazil began to process her own coffee instead of selling it raw to the U.S. By using a combination of cheap labour and poorer quality beans, she captured 14 per cent of the American market. In March 1968, the Brazilian Government was forced to impose a tax on her coffee, making the inferior local product as expensive to exporters as the best quality U.S. coffee. So America's continued domination of the market was safeguarded.

It is not only in her own backyard that the United States has flexed her muscles and sent some weakling nation flying, after first filching its wallet. In 1953, a C.I.A.-inspired plot got rid of Iran's Mossadegh when he threatened to nationalize the oil industry. Mr Mossadegh was not the most lovable of world leaders, but the C.I.A. managed to install in his place General Zahedi, whose reputation was even more dubious. The U.S. didn't give a damn about this; only the people had to live with him. He had one redeeming virtue, a nice sense of gratitude which he showed by leasing 40 per cent of Iranian oil to three U.S. companies.

And so it goes on. Poor nations, hopelessly sunk in poverty and misery, are pushed around by the Big Boys. Their governments are overthrown and despots foisted on the unwilling people; their national unity is undermined by the arming and financing of opposition factions, and they live within the shadow cast by the 6,000 military bases the United States maintains on other people's soil – a warning that what is good for the U.S. had better be good for the 'free' world – or else!

The old Spy Game is deader than the dodo. The Central Intelligence Agency long ago went beyond the stage of ferreting out another nation's secrets. By self-conferred authority, the C.I.A. reserves the right to make and break supposedly free governments to suit America's strategic and economic interests. And the criterion for mounting these modern epics of piracy is simple. 'Good' government is one which will play the international big business game even though it grinds the faces of its own poor and rules by terror. A government is 'bad', and ripe for subversion, even though truly democratic, if it tries to get out of the pit of international obligation and claims its own resources to feed its own people.

Of course, the United States does not play this game single-handed. As the Victorian music hall jingle had it, she's got the ships, she's got the men, she's got the money too, so she often acts on behalf of the rest of the *Unpoor* nations of the West who have abandoned those deadly rivalries which drove them to carve up Africa and parts of Asia in the nineteenth century. The new imperialism is truly international. Giant combines, financed jointly in the United States, Britain, West Germany, Italy, with a catholic dash of colour provided by Japan, are busy feeding upon the poor nations with a delicacy equal to that of the virtuoso surgeon who, according to legend, could remove a patient's heart without spilling a drop of his blood. Mortality was inevitable, alas, but it was such a neat job!

The Big Business Bogy with which communist agitators used to frighten the British working classes in the 1930s has become an awful reality in the poor world of the 1960s. When international tycoons swoop down on the new nations in their private jets, rulers fear for the integrity of their frontiers, the honesty of the public service, and the security of their own jobs. Yet they find it hard to resist the sales talk and the wealth which backs it, for they know they need capital and more capital if the cramped horizons of their people's lives are to be lifted. But is it worth it? That is the question which has Presidents and Prime Ministers pacing their bedroom floors at night.

They Call it Independence

There is no braver sight than a new nation sending up the fireworks and beating out its very own national anthem to celebrate independence. But it takes more than a piece of parchment and a national flag to protect it from outside interference if it owns anything that can be bought, sold, or exploited. Only those nations whose frontiers encompass arid wastelands can feel secure. They are simple charity cases, living like tick birds on the crocodile's back, safe because they are unappetizing.

Any young nation that imagines it will be left in peace to enjoy whatever treasure God has given it should ponder the sorry lesson of the Congo which, on the eve of independence in 1960, was the nominal owner of some of the world's wealthiest mineral deposits, mostly concentrated in the Katanga province. Under Belgian rule the mining industry was run by a board on which the State had a two-thirds majority. Three days before independence the Belgians dissolved the board to prevent the Congolese inheriting a controlling interest in their own mines, and organized a re-distribution of shares to give a private Belgian company an 180,000 share majority over the State. Independence was to be skin deep only; the people could have the land, but the untold wealth under the earth had the Belgian flag pasted across it.

Then came the rough stuff. During an episode as squalid as any in Africa's history, an operation was mounted to split off the wealthy Katanga from the rest of the Congo and run it as a semi-dependency of Belgium under the puppet Moise Tsombe. The plot was exposed by the Chairman of the Brussels Stock Exchange who, at the end of 1960, declared with guileless candour, 'The Congo has escaped from our hands but we can still save the Katanga with its cobalt, tin, zinc, copper, and uranium mines. If Katanga slips out too, the shares of *Union Miniere du Haut Katanga* will go down. If the Belgians stay in the Congo the shares will double in value . . .'*

To deny the Congolese their heritage every sordid trick was used. The murder of Patrice Lumumba – the only leader with an outside chance of uniting the Congo – the inflaming of old tribal hatreds and the employment of white mercenary armies resulted in a devil's stew which finally embroiled the United

*Quoted by L. Goncharov, in *Modern African Studies*, Cambridge, Vol. 1, No. 4, p. 469.

Nations, Britain, the United States, Russia, and China. And the Congolese have gone on paying the bill with their blood in anarchy, mass murder, and chronic political instability. But as they say in the West, with breathtaking gall, that's what happens when you give a nation independence too soon!

France, too, with Gallic subtlety, trussed up her former colonies so tightly that independence meant little more than the freedom to wiggle a little finger. They were to remain suppliers of raw materials and tropical foodstuffs to France whilst serving as a closed market for her goods. Using an elaborate network of agencies with fancy initials – FIDES, FAC, CCCE – the French arranged to transfer money from one pocket to the other, getting it silver-coated on its journey through Africa. To begin with, 80 per cent of France's investment in her former African colonies returns to her in the form of payments for materials, services, and salaries of French staff and agents. Good business indeed, but it is stretching language to call such a cosy financial operation 'aid'.

Mr Walter Rostow, a former U.S. State Department official, let the cat out of the bag in an interview with *U.S. News and World Report* when he called foreign aid 'a means of buying time to protect crucial pieces of real estate'. He added, 'In playing the game in an underdeveloped area you must be prepared to play for a long time.' Some game! A jolly little romp for all concerned except the poor people who put up the biggest stakes – their lives and the lives of their children – with no chance of a prize bigger than bare survival.

The poor cannot win. However they twist and turn they are unable to free themselves from the sticky webs of international obligation in which they are trapped. Grinding labour does not put more bread in their mouths, for by the strange operation of some nightmare economic law, the harder they work, the less they earn. World markets are rigged in such a way that the goods which poor nations produce – cotton, rubber, cocoa, sugar, tea, and base metals – sell for less and less at a time when the prices of manufactured goods the rich nations supply to them have rocketed upwards.

In 1954, Ghana produced 210,000 long tons of cocoa which fetched £85½ million on world markets. In 1965 she increased production to 590,000 long tons of cocoa, but only earned £70 million for the crop. Brazil's coffee production increased by 90 per cent between 1953 and 1961, yet her earnings from it fell by 35 per cent. According to one economist, Susan Strange,* in the eight years 1955–63 poor nations earned 12½ per cent less for their goods in spite of great production increases, but had to pay 16 per cent more for the things they bought from the rich nations. Such statistics spell lunacy to the detached observer, prosperity to the rich, and despair to the poor.

A U.S. Senator speaking in Congress is reported to have based his argument in support of foreign aid on the belief that what America lost on the swings she would more than gain on the roundabouts. He said a mouthful. Falling prices of raw materials the United States buys from Latin America more than compensate for the aid she sends to the area. Britain makes a profit on her aid to the Argentine. France sucked Vietnam dry until Ho Chi Minh booted her out in 1954. Not since the days of the truck system when coal miners were forced to buy the necessities of life from company 'tommy' shops at inflated prices has such a foolproof method of revaluing money been invented. The dollar which is fat with value in the hand of the rich seems mysteriously to

*Quoted by Segal, *The Race War*, Penguin, 1967.

shrivel when the poor get hold of it. Possibly there is no evil genius behind it all. Possibly the universe is a cosmically capitalist system where, by the tranquil operation of perpetual providence, as the collect puts it, the rich cannot help getting richer and the poor are expected to cheer them on – if so, Heaven is overdue a revolution.

A Three-Letter Word Meaning Fraud

At present, the *Unpoor*, screaming outrage all the while, spend about half of one per cent of their income on something they call aid. They protest that this commitment is wringing them dry and are cutting it down every year. Meanwhile they purchase an illusory security at a cost of thirty times their aid bill from armaments whose rate of obsolescence is so great that the countryside is littered with rusting aircraft and out-dated weapons. There is obviously no honour amongst thieves. The rich live in terror of their fellow robbers, presumably, for if they feared the wrath of the poor the investment of their military budgets in genuine aid would buy more security than the most powerful weaponry.

Aid is often a three-letter word meaning fraud. A loan is not aid if the poor nation has to sink deeper into debt paying it off. Money which must be spent in the donor country on goods the giver stipulates is not aid but a roundabout way of subsidizing the rich country's industries. Grants are not aid but Pieces of Silver if the country which receives them must put up with foreign troops on her soil or enter into defence pacts which require precious money to be spent on supersonic jets whilst peasants scratch the earth with sticks for lack of steel ploughs. It is not aid but war-mongering to offer a poor country easier payment terms for tanks and military aircraft than for harvesters and trucks.

A country which holds out one hand for help often finds the other twisted behind its back in a half-nelson to force prompt obedience when the whip is cracked. There is no such thing as aid without strings. President Johnson, who is not noted for his diplomatic polish, said once that he would only give aid to countries which were not hostile to the United States and which showed solid evidence of being prepared to help themselves. It had apparently slipped his mind what happened to Brazil when she tried to help herself to a fair share of the coffee market. But poor nations long ago learned the imperialist's argot. The President's words, being interpreted, meant that to be found worthy of a share of the great dollar bonanza a poor nation must make suitable anti-communist growling noises, avoid trespassing on U.S. markets, and help itself deeper into debt – all the while madly waving the Stars and Stripes and smiling broadly for the benefit of *Time-Life* photographers.

Any poor nation that dares to be truly free has the aspect of bankrupt premises. Ask President Nyerere of Tanzania. First he lost American money because he brought in a handful of Chinese technicians. Then West Germany cut off all aid when he refused to expel the East German consul in Zanzibar. Finally Britain stopped £7 million worth of aid because Tanzania broke off diplomatic relations with her over Rhodesia. Is the primary purpose of aid to fill hungry mouths or to buy acquiescence? Tanzanians went on being hungry because of a squabble between two Governments carried on at a level way beyond their ken. However resigned one is to the fact that Britain gets more petulant as her moral stature declines, to cut off aid to a poor nation out of pique was a childish and immoral act comparable to punishing a serf by putting his children on bread and water because he failed to touch his forelock to the squire. There is a robust, old-fashioned villainy about the *Unpoor* that is so staggering it almost disarms criticism.

Russia's record is little better than that of the West, though until the invasion of Czechoslovakia she operated with more finesse. For years the great People's Republic has forced her Eastern satellites to buy goods from her at inflated prices, and has taken their goods for a song. Cuba, rebounding in fury from the American Capitalist Ogre into the arms of Russia, found herself having to pay prices well above world averages for the manufactured goods she took in exchange for her sugar. When it comes to the exploitation of the poor, distinctions between capitalists and socialists vanish. It is the *Unpoor* versus the rest.

Probably the world's poor have been most cynically betrayed by the so-called left-wingers in Western democracies who protest the evils of the capitalist system and yet avoid like the plague doing anything to weaken it. Britain's Labourites rise to their feet at the end of every Party Conference and, looking as sheepish as bishops watching a strip show, bellow forth those stirring words, 'Let cowards flinch and traitors sneer, We'll keep the Red Flag flying here!' But for all the beery trade union rhetoric about international brotherhood, their record as a Government proves that the delights of socialism stop at Dover. If the world's poor do not know it already, they will soon learn that the socialists are not worth half a dozen more crusts in starving mouths than the Tories, who to their credit do not preach revolution whilst entrenching national selfishness. At least Tory aid is an honest dole from the unapologetically privileged;

it is not garnished with slush about workers' solidarity and human dignity.

The poor must look elsewhere for salvation, and their straining eyes detect a kind of light dawning beyond the Himalayas. China, the greatest of the historically underdeveloped nations, has, in spite of American harassment and the withdrawal of Russian support, jumped into the forefront of the industrial advanced countries and is beginning to help her own kind. She has pledged more than $1,500 million in aid to North Korea, two thirds of which has been claimed, and by 1964 had given $500 million to other poor nations. This aid is more than money, it is a symbol foreshadowing the self-reliance of the poor world and an end to dependence upon the favours of the West.

In China, the poor world has discovered a champion who rose from their own ranks and has a common history of exploitation and discrimination. She has grown mighty by the efforts of her own people, and is too powerful to be pushed around by the West. A price will have to be paid for unity on China's terms which liberal democracies would find daunting, but at least the poor nations will get back the most precious thing that has been stolen from them – their self-respect.

Dig your way under the mountain of facts and statistics and one simple truth is laid bare. The *Unpoor* have grown fat on a rotten social and economic system held together by force, robbery, and exploitation. And they are happy to keep it that way.

Whilst fifty-five million people starve to death each year, the *Unpoor* squander astronomic sums on advertising to tickle the jaded appetities of their overstuffed people. Britain spends six times more on advertising than overseas aid. Her people must be enticed to eat, drink, smoke, and wear more, to find room in their groaning bellies for another candy bar. It is all part of the pain of wealth, to be bombarded by the competing claims of different brands of trash. The most appropriate monument to the *Unpoor* will be erected from the tons of discarded soap flake and breakfast cereal boxes and squeezed-out toothpaste tubes carried away every day by the corporation dustmen.

It cannot last. No society whose values are so warped and tawdry will survive indefinitely. Replete, under-exercised, neurotic, and bored, the *Unpoor* are ill-equipped for the world struggle which has already started. A long time ago, H. G. Wells, in his novel *The Man on the Moon*, wrote:

> It dawned upon me up there in the moon a thing I ought always to have known, that man is not made simply to go about being safe and comfortable, and well fed and amused. Against his interest, against his happiness, he is constantly being driven to do unreasonable things....

The *Unpoor* steadfastly refuse to do unreasonable things which clash with their self-interest, for this is capitalism's Sin against the Holy Ghost. It is the gospel of utter reasonableness, of cause and effect, input and output, investment and return. As a system, its cogs mesh together so snugly that there are no gaps through which a little mercy might seep out. But capitalism, in the last resort, by the compensations of some kind of justice, strengthens only those upon whom it lays intolerable burdens, and saps the life force of the ones who derive their ease and comfort from it. That is why the *Unpoor* are in bad shape for the future.

Raspberry Among the Hallelujahs
I have no defence against the charge that this account of the *Unyoung*, *Uncoloured*, and *Unpoor* is viciously one-sided, nor would I be interested in offering one. When someone has his knee in your groin, you are not required to do justice to the colour of his eyes or take into account the fact that he dotes on his wife and children. Anyway, the Devil has all the best tunes and most of the best singers. The rulers of this world pay an army of professional white-washers to feed their limitless appetite for self-congratulation. One raspberry is not going to drown out the chorus of hallelujahs.

The problem is that Up-People are impossible to parody. Just when you think you have sketched a passable caricature of them you realize that your malice has been wasted; unwittingly you've told the God-awful truth. Ridicule falters before their terrible solemnity – tell them the joke about 'the young lady of Riga who went for a ride on a tiger' and they will endow a Foundation to investigate the phenomenon. Their world may seem rock-solid, but they flit through it like ghosts, in essence totally elusive. Reach for their heart and you have hold of a joke parcel you can go on unwrapping for ever. Reading their mind is like thumbing through a glossy magazine in a foreign language – slickly uninforming. Only if you wave a pound note in front of their eyes are you rewarded by a recognizable flicker.

Their values are so inane that they are no more an effective check upon the fantastic power at their disposal than a wrapping of Christmas paper round an elephant. They talk; their mouths open and sentences tumble out that serve only to punctuate the silence. By their bumbling, they have so trivialized honest emotion that words like sacrifice, love, and duty have to be scrubbed with disinfectant before they can be spoken without a sneer.

They will have to be smashed because they cannot be changed. Getting to grips with what they believe is like trying to bite a fat balloon. It is impossible to pick a fight with them about their convictions, for rather than suffer inconvenience they will abandon them and shop around for another set. So tensionless are they that if archaeologists dug up proof that Jesus was the fictitious creation of a gang of Galilean confidence tricksters, they would still troop into church on Sunday unperturbed, feeling that something so innately decent as the Jesus-idea was worth a weekly nod. Their convictions about almost anything, except money, are little more than a reflex, the twitching of a compass needle in the vague direction of some moral pole.

Radical ideas will never reshape their society. What Mr Wilson's Government has done to socialism, and the Western Church to Jesus, they would do with equal ease to any radicalism, political or religious – believe a bit and spit out the rest. They can, at will, reverse the miracle at Cana and turn wine into water, absorbing strong ideas without trace in a mish-mash of dirty grey moderation. They destroy their detractors by clasping them fondly to their bosoms and asphyxiating them. They are so decadent as to make ancient Byzantium seem like the New Jerusalem and yet so decent that even when they are clubbing you to death you feel impelled to apologize for spilling blood on their carpet.

CHAPTER FIVE

THE SACRED COW OF NON-VIOLENCE

NOTHING short of revolution will cauterize the stinking sores of the West. A fair slice of the Christian world is agreed about that – the Vatican, the World Council of Churches, bishops, theologians, and parish pump preachers. By revolution they mean many things, all important; drastic reform of the Church, more dynamic Christian witness, a new spirit in men's hearts – but they do *not* mean blood, bombs, and barricades. As European Marxists are fond of saying, and the use of talking shop jargon goes a long way to explain their ineffectiveness, violence is not on the agenda in the West.

Christians of strong passions who are bursting with indignation at the injustice of things turn increasingly to passive resistance as a weapon of which they think Jesus would approve. Non-violence is being hailed as the greatest innovation in human conflict since the invention of gunpowder. Like the modern insecticide, it is supposed to be both powerfully effective and harmless to human beings. Disciples of peaceful protest have already written a glowing page in the history books by their courage in submitting to police brutality, imprisonment, and sometimes death without lifting a finger in retaliation.

Martyrdom is difficult to argue against. Yet it is possible to be wrong-headed even when one's heart is in the right place. Non-violent revolution is like nonalcoholic wine, a symbol of sorts but a poor substitute for the real thing. And this, not only because an oppressive system ribbed with cold steel is unlikely to dissolve in the hot tears of vicarious pain, nor because the great revolutions of modern times – Britain (1640), America (1776), France (1789), Russia (1917), and China (1948) – demanded violence on a large scale. The problem is that the purest actions can have calamitous consequences in a bent world. There's an Italian saying: spit in the Arno and you'll cause waves at Pisa. As a revolutionary, the passive resister is like a man who blows up a hideous block of flats under the illusion that he alone will be injured by the falling masonry. With heart overflowing with love and slightly less aggressive than a new-born lamb, he still causes a blood-bath.

Prophets of Non-Violence

The passive resistance movement claims three men as its prophets – Jesus, Schweitzer and Gandhi. Jesus must have a chapter to himself because, as a Christian writing to another Christian, my argument stands or falls by his attitude to violence. For the time being I only comment that if we go by the strict letter of the gospels, neither violent nor non-violent revolutionaries can put Jesus into the witness box on their behalf. He would have no truck with any kind of resistance to evil. Paul Ramsey, summarizing Jesus' attitude to the use of force, writes: 'Non-resistance is incommensurable with *any* form of resistance. Resistance does not become any more Christian by being non-violent, neither is armed resistance unchristian by virtue of being armed but by virtue of its being resistant . . .'*

Jesus softened none of his harsh absolutes to allow

*Ramsey, *Basic Christian Ethics*, S.C.M., 1953, p. 68.

for peaceful alternatives to violence. He did not say you must turn the other cheek when provoked *but* you can form a passive human barrier against the police. He did not say you ought not to resist evil *but* you can burn draft cards. He did not say you must love your neighbour *but* you can hold a sit-in on his property or boycott his products. The passive resister may feel that to force an issue by bringing suffering upon himself is a cleaner and more spiritual way than that of the guerrilla fighter, but Jesus never said so.

Albert Schweitzer is a curious choice of *guru* for the passive resistance movement. Reverence for Life, that truth which struck him with the blinding force of a revelation as he made his way down the Ogowe River in 1915, certainly urges that we shrink from harming anything that lives, plant, insect, or human being. In his *Civilisation and Ethics*, Schweitzer describes the truly ethical man:

> Life as such is sacred. He tears no leaf from a tree, plucks no flowers and takes care to crush no insect. If in summer he is working by lamplight, he prefers to keep the window shut and breathe the stuffy atmosphere rather than see one insect after another fall with singed wings upon his table. . . . Ethics are responsibility without limit to all that lives . . .

That is finely said, but it preaches the kind of tolerance which is a great enemy of revolution. Here is the passivity of the Hindu who will not lift a finger to destroy a diseased cow or a vile caste system. Schweitzer was a man of many parts and never claimed that politics was one of them, but the colonial territory in which he lived was a classical setting for putting Reverence for Life to work politically. And it is a matter of record that the Doctor of Lamberéné who took great pains to avoid stepping on an ant in his path was strangely insensitive to the Gabonese people's dignity, bruised by the denial of their political rights. When the Gabon got its independence in 1960, he showed the grumpiness of a grizzly bear towards its African rulers and pined aloud for the old order of things. Reverence for Life, widely practised, would make the world more humane but hardly more just. It refines man's spirit at the cost of sapping his will to root out and destroy whatever brutalizes him.

Mohandas Karamchad Gandhi has a much stronger claim to being the father of the passive resistance movement. He was the first popular leader to turn non-violence into a large-scale political weapon, and it is significant that he first used it in South Africa, still under British rule but already sliding away towards *apartheid.* He claimed that his doctrine of *satyagraha* – firmness in the truth – was Christian in inspiration. 'It was the New Testament which really awakened me to the rightness and value of passive resistance,' he wrote in 1908. Maybe it did; but his talk of violence as 'body force' as opposed to the 'soul force' of non-violence has more the ring of Plato than Jesus about it, giving a face-lift to the old heresy that the 'spiritual' is good whilst the 'physical' is evil. As the spear-head of India's freedom struggle, Gandhi used the technique with great flair, persuading thousands to join him in civil disobedience, boycott, and hunger strike. However, his story exposes the weaknesses of *satyagraha* as an exclusive alternative to the use of force in revolution.

The holy man in the India of Gandhi's time enjoyed great authority. Even those who, because of much wealth or abject poverty, were eaten away by a squalid materialism acknowledge the supremacy of spiritual values they could not themselves attain. This spindle-legged saint, crafty with goodness, commanded a loyalty no purely political leader could get or deserve. For those who saw in him the embodiment of truth, the tougher he made things the more earnest their efforts to match him. Like all great religious leaders, Gandhi asked of his devotees the unexpected, the unnatural, the paradoxical. To fast to death outside the Viceroy's palace; to invite angry police to rain down *lathi* blows without striking back; to take a forbidden pinch of salt from the sea at Dandi and sit quietly awaiting arrest: these were, in Gandhi's eyes, tests of spiritual athleticism. He and his followers were buoyed up on India's large soul, fed for thousands of years by her religion. By contrast, the soul of the West has the texture and dimensions of a wrinkled walnut. Those who hope to draw spiritual power from it for a purifying non-violent struggle will find in it the nourishment of that soup of which Dickens wrote, made from the shadow of a very small pigeon which had died of starvation.

In the British Raj, Gandhi faced not a ruthless dictator but a bumbling, well-meaning, shaky overlord whose attitude towards him dithered between finger-wagging headmasterly sternness and fond indulgence. Magistrates prefaced their sentences with elaborate speeches of regret; Viceroys and Colonial Secretaries made pilgrimage to the prisons he was dignifying by his presence, bearing as gifts books by his favourite authors and a few choice tit-bits of whatever his spartan diet would allow. He was permitted to make press statements from his cell, pleading his case to the world. Newsreel cameras recorded the sufferings of his followers. Either through the high-mindedness or ineptitude of his opponents, he was able to make political capital out of his privations. Passive resistance depends for its success upon the creation of a public opinion which will be shamed or angered into giving justice to those who choose to match official power with self-sacrifice. Gandhi had no possible complaint on this score. British tolerance plus Hindu fanaticism was a winning combination.

Ruthless modern despots do not play good-natured games with their critics. It is hard to imagine Hitler or Stalin blenching at the prospect of Gandhi fasting to death. They would have helped him on his way, exterminating him secretly so that there was no mark of his passing except for a blood stain on some cellar wall. Had Gandhi been got rid of in this way, the moral value of his sacrifice might still stand for all time, but its political significance would have shrunk to nothing. People who vanish without trace do not make effective rallying-points for freedom. Thousands of men of peace who refused to bow the knee to Baal filed through the gates of Nazi concentration camps and disappeared for ever: one moment, they were; the next, they were not. Only after the monstrous tyranny had been smashed by force were their courage and nobility revealed to the world – too late, alas, to affect the course of events. In the sight of God, those who die for what is right may shine brighter than the stars of heaven, but unknown martyrdoms make poor political beacon lights.

Diamond on Black Velvet

Stripped of its dramatic overtones, passive resistance is an exercise in public relations. Unfortunately, this means fighting Establishments on their own ground, for even when they will not stoop to the garotte and gas chamber, they can manipulate mass media to tell any story their way and point up the moral which will put them in the best possible light. This is precisely what happened to the Great Vietnam Protest March through London in October 1968. A gesture of agonized concern was grotesquely twisted by clever propaganda. The march organizers were out-manoeuvred in such a way that they could not win at any price. Had the forty thousand marchers become a disorderly rabble, the collapse of non-violent protest would have been proclaimed to the world. In the event, there were few violent incidents and the crowd kept cool, for which the police, and not the march leaders, got the public credit; newspapers and television commentators rhapsodized their patience, discipline, and lack of brutality. What started as a massive vote of no-confidence in the Government ended to the fanfare of trumpets as a triumph for true democracy, generous enough to permit mass protest and efficient enough to frustrate it.

Something like the same fate overtook the Hunger March on Washington. When the last of the marchers finally abandoned Resurrection City, their temporary shanty town, the Federal Government made the whole thing look faintly ridiculous by politely sending the organizers a bill for $70,000, the cost of clearing up litter left behind by the protestors. There were, however, few sneers on the faces of Officialdom earlier that same year as they surveyed the blackened skeleton of the Detroit ghetto, burnt out by Negro rioters. Not even the slickest public relations machine could rob of menace the terrible truth told by those devastated buildings.

The most important lesson to be learned from Gandhi's story is that non-violent resistance, far from being an alternative to the use of force, only becomes politically significant against a background of widespread violence. Like a diamond, it needs black velvet to set it off. Gandhi's faith in passive resistance never wavered, but the Indian National Congress finally abandoned the policy in 1935, turning to direct action. By 1942, Gandhi had lost political control of all but a handful of his followers, and civil war raged throughout India – Britain using tanks and even aircraft to keep order. Yet during the seven years that Gandhi was in the political wilderness, able to speak for no national movement, his stock reached new heights with the British Government. Passive resistance was no longer an amiable eccentricity on Gandhi's part; it had become the lesser of two evils. So long as the Indian National Congress was committed to non-violence, its demands were brushed aside, and Gandhi's warnings went unheeded. Only when most Indian leaders realized they were wasting their time hoping that by getting beaten up often enough they would win did the British Government begin to take Gandhi seriously. But even as Viceroys listened respectfully to the Mahatma's statesman-like words, their ears were attuned to the clamour of the rioting mob off-stage. To win a hearing, the leader of peaceful protest must be able to say, in effect, 'My way – or this!', pointing to mounting chaos.

Kwame Nkrumah once said, 'Freedom has never been handed on a silver platter to any colonial territory; it has been won only after bitter and vigorous struggles.' History bears him out – Egypt, Indonesia, Cyprus, Israel, the Congo, Algeria, Kenya. Nationalist leaders learned long ago that this is a fact of life. Those officially committed to non-violence discovered that the way to win concessions was to point out to the colonial power that their followers, whose mayhem they sometimes secretly encouraged, were getting out of hand. Most nationalist movements had their militant wing, publicly frowned upon but privately blessed for spelling out for the authorities the lurid alternative to sweet reasonableness.

The career of Martin Luther King is a good illustration of the necessary counterpointing of violence with non-violence. In the years immediately following the 1954 Montgomery Bus Boycott which catapulted King to fame, he was a social outcast from white circles and his pleas on behalf of his own people were largely ignored. When a new generation of Negro militants appeared to his left – Malcolm X, Rap Brown, Stokely Carmichael – the authorities suddenly discovered King's value to them. He was fêted, lionized, invited to the White House, proclaimed a statesman, and contrasted with the rabble rousers and hate preachers of Black Power. Yet the Negro apostles of non-violent protest owed their influence with the Government to the ghetto militants in the same way the moon owes its pale light to a fiery sun. Martin Luther King's powerful advocacy of the Gospel of Love tinkled sweetly on the ears of U.S. President and people in comparison with Stokely Carmichael's uncompromising declaration, 'Black people should and must fight back. Nothing more quickly repels someone bent on destroying you than the unequivocal message, "O.K. Fool! Make your move, and run the same risk as I do, of dying!" ' With superb courage and high faith, Martin Luther King marched his men, like the Grand Old Duke of York, up the hill and down again for years, but it was the firing of the Negro ghettos which rocked Capitol Hill on its foundations. Doors that King and his followers had knocked upon without success suddenly yielded to the hefty kick of Negro militancy.

I am not denying passive resistance its due place in the freedom struggle, or belittling the contribution to it of men like Gandhi and Martin Luther King. Both have a secure place in history. I merely want to show that however much the disciples of passive resistance detest violence, they are politically impotent without it. American Negroes needed both Martin Luther King and Malcolm X, just as India had to have both Gandhi and Nehru. Either method of forcing an issue becomes self-defeating if used at the wrong time and in the wrong way. Passive resistance movements may strengthen the Authority they seek to challenge if they act as a lightning rod, diverting into safe and manageable channels the explosive energy of the people's just anger. Badly directed violence may, at great cost in human life, give Authority an excuse to rid itself once and for all of thorns in its flesh.

Just as there is a time to speak and a time to keep silent, so there is a time to fight and a time to resist by other means. This is not so much a moral choice as a tactical one. I have heard it claimed that the peaceful harassment of Soviet troops by Czech patriots in Prague during the recent invasion was a triumphant vindication of passive resistance. Hardly a triumph, for what did it change? But it was the only sane response to sudden and overwhelming military aggression and, therefore, the correct response. On another day, or under different conditions, guerrilla warfare might be the one way of preventing an invader from settling down in comfort to enjoy the fruits of conquest. Tactics dictate the weapon. And if someone retorts that this is playing fast and loose with ethics, confusing means and ends, remember Lenin's reply when told that the end does not justify the means. 'What else does?' he asked.

It skates over an important issue to say that passive

resistance or violence should be used as the occasion demands. The passive resister and the revolutionary are not, generally speaking, similar personality types. Each, when roused, does what it is in his nature to do. It is as hard for the one to kill as for the other to suffer without striking back. More than this, there is the Class aspect. In spite of Gandhi and his ragged legions of Untouchables, passive resistance is a middle-class phenomenon, engaged in by those who have comfort and security to lose. And it is important that the authorities they are resisting should be aware of the extent of their sacrifice, for this is the nub of the moral pressure being brought to bear. Passive resistance does not work where those who resist and those being resisted have different values and attitudes to life. A Latin American military governor would realize that a doctor or lawyer felt strongly about an issue if they were willing to be clubbed down by his troops in the course of a demonstration; he, too, would hate to exchange a comfortable and gracious life for a gaol cell. He would not get the same message if poor peasants submitted willingly to being brutalized, since it is little change from their daily lot anyway. The passive resister has no lever from which to apply pressure if the authorities are oblivious of the fact that he is risking anything that really matters to him.

This is why the wretched of the earth do not go in for passive resistance. It is no novelty for them to suffer without retaliation, but the sorry story of their daily lives, and they want an end to it. Nor, unlike the passive resister, can they settle for a moral victory. Having nerved themselves to strike a blow, it must be decisive because they know they are unlikely to get a second chance. They can expect no protection from the law, from wealth, or from a tradition of fair play. They have few qualms about using violence because society as they know it is a system of organized violence. In a fight to the death, they have so little to lose that they have the advantage over those who have much to lose. For example, in political terms, the death of one Vietcong is not equal to the death of one U.S. serviceman. It is his house, car, wealth, job, life-expectancy, in the balance against a bowl of rice and a handful of rags and precious little else.

Possibly protein-starved brains are unable to grasp the sophisticated ideas behind passive resistance, or else the repressed classes' philosophy of life has no room for the belief that right must eventually prevail in a moral universe. Those for whom life is nasty, brutish, and short are unlikely to survive long enough to benefit from the slow grinding of the Mills of God.

The Heart of the Matter

How are Christians to be convinced that their precious moral distinction between violence and non-violence is often a delusion? I must qualify that. There are Christian perfectionists who have contracted right out of the world in order to witness to an impossible ideal – absolute pacifists, monks, members of apocalyptic communities living in daily expectation of the Lord's return, to mention some. They will have nothing to do with force in any shape or form, legal or otherwise. In their case there *is* a moral distinction between violence and non-violence. They deserve every respect, provided their idealism does not degenerate into muddle-headedness through trying to build a political platform upon individual perfection.

For the rest; any Christian is entitled to say he will not use violence. That is a matter for his own conscience. But it is sheer priggishness to behave as though his personal conviction were a general rule and to judge others accordingly. Most passive resisters live within, and benefit from, a social system based upon force. As Emil Brunner has written: 'He who affirms the State, affirms violence.' In a sinful world, justice in society can only take the form of balancing the competing interests of every member by the use of coercion. The Christian may never draw a sword, but others will have to do so on his behalf, and by accepting the rights and duty of citizenship he is assenting to this state of affairs. In these circumstances, for him to say that he will have nothing to do with violence is like a fish swimming through the ocean and loudly proclaiming that water is evil.

The revolutionary's quarrel with the passive resister is that he is content to be in the world until the crunch comes, then he suddenly discovers that he is not of it. Having accepted the rules of the earthly game, the passive resister wants to import one of the laws of heaven and become a perfectionist on a single issue – the outlawing of violence as a method of getting justice. It does not ring true. A great deal of violence, with and without the force of law, has been used to carve out the good life he enjoys, yet he frowns upon others using the same means to get a decent life for themselves. He sympathizes with the oppressed of the earth and accepts the need for a revolution to establish human dignity, but he adds, of course, '*No* violence!' for that would be morally wrong and, therefore, self-defeating. But it is far from obvious to those he is exhorting that violence *is* self-defeating since they can see that most of what *he* has is owed to violence and protected by it.

Because the passive resister lives within an over-all situation of violence, his hope that he can change things without anyone getting hurt is an illusion. Policemen are often injured and property destroyed in the course of non-violent mass demonstrations. When Gandhi decided as a peaceful measure to boycott English cotton goods, Lancashire children went hungry as a result. The British Prime Minister, in announcing that he would not use force against Rhodesia but the more humane policy of sanctions, was still driving black Rhodesian farm labourers and their families to starvation point. I am not saying that any of these measures was wrong; merely that those who use them should not take refuge in a false sense of virtue. The Christian who chooses responsibly the way of revolution knows that he is going to hurt people, and is horrified at the prospect. The passive resister, on the other hand, may not be personally responsible for hurting anyone, but he must not fool himself. He will still be the occasion of others' sinning as they use force to meet his challenge. There are no such things as political strategies which are both innocent and effective.

No More Excellent Way?

In attempting to shatter an unjust and corrupt system the practical choice is rarely between passive resistance and an armed freedom struggle, but more likely between the freedom struggle and world war. To take your own case, if Rhodesian freedom fighters fail in their objectives, sooner or later Great Powers will clash in Southern Africa. Terrorism, however much we detest the cruel implications of the term, is not a degenerate form of war but an alternative to it. The selective brutality of terrorism is to be preferred to the impartial horrors of war. A freedom struggle offers the possibility, however slight, of localizing an inevitable conflict without enlisting the great power blocs which will collide across the world.

Albert Camus, in an essay written in 1946, *Neither Victims Nor Executioners*, put the opposing point of view, and rules out revolution altogether on the grounds that it must lead to general war, which means a nuclear holocaust. This argument suits the West admirably. It implies that because Western powers happened to have the Bomb when the whistle was blown to signal the end of all national contests, they can lean on non-nuclear nations with a sense of moral superiority. If Asian peasants resist Western imperialism by force they are presumably responsible at the bar of history should someone in Washington or Moscow press the red button and take the world off its hinges. This is like saying that a mouse ought not to bite the paw of a lion crushing it to death for fear the angry predator will tear its cage apart.

The freedom fighter, whether he operates in the Zambesi Valley or a Chicago ghetto, is not introducing violence into a peaceful society. He is responding pathetically to a greater violence which is not less murderous because it is clothed in the majesty of the law. Western society is not at peace – it is in an uneasy state of equilibrium achieved by the deployment of massive force against mass indignation. To starve people is violence; to rob them of their dignity and self-respect is violence; to deny them political rights or discriminate against them is violence. Elaborate structures of violence make a terrorist what he is, and he faces them as the weaker adversary. He matches mobility against strength, the element of surprise against powerful formations, meagre resources against great concentrations of force, sharpened bamboo stakes and small arms against the flame-thrower and the napalm bomb. Terrorism is the only means by which desperate men can dramatize their grievances in a system which controls all the media of education and communication and uses them without scruple to distort the truth about human suffering. Other than the weapons of the impotent, the terrorist has only a single advantage – he has so little to lose that death in the jungle is not much worse than life in a hovel. The system can deny him the right to live like a man, but it cannot stop him from dying like one.

Of course, it is impossibly difficult to reconcile Christ's command that we should love our neighbour with the decision to destroy him. But the initial violation of that commandment has occurred long before the first desperate man picks up a stone or fires a shot. When a whole system is based on the denial of love, it is futile to counsel the victims of monstrous injustice to possess their souls in patience because the coming of God's Kingdom will put things right. The statement issued in 1957 by sixteen Roman Catholic bishops to the people of the Third World on *The Gospel and Revolution* ends with the ringing words of Jesus, 'Look up and raise your heads because your redemption draws near.' The more cynical of the unhappy masses addressed might well retort that supernatural help has been drawing near for two thousnd years and still hasn't arrived. Why should they believe that the Great Day will dawn tomorrow? Does the affluent West with its insurance policies and long-term economic plans act upon that assumption? Pious talk of awaiting a Kingdom beyond history comes easily to the warm and well-fed. They won't find the delay too arduous. But in the brute battle for survival, every day is an eternity. Who can blame the down-trodden for feeling they must act now, and damn the consequences?

And yet the words and witness of Jesus stick in the throat of any Christian contemplating revolution. He who was a stumbling-block to Jews and foolishness to the Greeks is an Almighty Headache to the Christian activist. What are we to make of Jesus' attitude to violence?

CHAPTER SIX

WHAT WOULD JESUS DO?

In the letter which sparked off this diatribe, you are asking in effect what Jesus would do in your situation. The truth is we do not know what he would do. In spite of the millions of words written and spoken about him, we know precious little about Jesus of Nazareth. The Gospels are pure propaganda, written by men who had some very large axes to grind; which is not to say that the four accounts of Jesus have no basis in fact, far from it. The problem is: which bits are historically true – those which suit my argument or those which demolish it? Effective propaganda is always the judicious selection of facts rather than the telling of bare-faced lies. The lies are easy to expose; the difficulty is to get at the truth which remains untold.

Once Jesus falls into the hands of the theologians he emerges barely recognizable, and we find ourselves moving, almost without landmarks, in a world of sanctified imagination. A Galilean peasant becomes the Cosmic Christ; his earthly life is a mere incident in an eternity-long existence; his death the key to a universal scheme of salvation. It is a magnificently elaborate theoretical construct which depends upon an Alice-in-Wonderland use of language and whose truth is a matter of faith not so much in God as in the Big Brains. You ought to believe it, say the theologians, bashing you over the head with Augustine, Aquinas, Luther, and

Calvin, because cleverer men than you have done. The trouble is, of course, that cleverer men than me have also disbelieved it, or believed something quite different.

If you once step outside the charmed circle of intellectual freemasonry, many of the doctrinal statements about Jesus have the aspect of a castle of cards, terribly vulnerable to a whiff or two of common sense. How, for example, without twisting words out of shape, do we answer the simple charge against the God-Man dogma that if Jesus was God he couldn't sin, and if he was Man he couldn't help it because perfection is impossible within history? The old heretics, far from leading the faithful astray, sometimes seemed to be striking a blow for truth when they let some daylight into the theological world of private meaning. Hadn't the Arians, for instance, got something when they jibed that if Jesus was a Being eternally co-existent with the Father, this must make him God's brother and not his son?

This Jesus of History some theologians chat about as though he were an old pal is a lay-figure built up of myth, dogma, guesswork, and pious supposition wrapped round a flimsy skeleton of fact. Hobbes said a mouthful when he claimed that coming to terms with Christianity is like taking a pill; if you swallow it in one gulp it will probably work, but start to chew it and you end up retching all over the place.

The preacher's Jesus often enough steps down out of a world of sheer fantasy to woo Sunday congregations. I blush when I recall the cockiness with which I have blasted forth the hidden thoughts of Jesus or confidently declared what he would do in hypothetical situations. Those sermonic meanderings of Jesus through the complex issues of our time are often little more than an ingenious preacher's guess as to how the nicest guy he can imagine would behave in similar circumstances.

So we don't know enough about Jesus either to locate him in the van of the revolution egging on the peasantry or to interpose him between the mob and the barricades pleading with murderous men to turn the other cheek. But in view of the claims made for him as the great advocate of non-violence, it is a little ironic that the only hard fact about his life corroborated by non-Christian historians of the time is that he was executed as a Jewish nationalist for stirring up rebellion against the Roman government of Judea. The Gospellers' attempt to prove this charge false and establish Jesus as the innocent dupe of crafty ecclesiastical foxes rings so hollow it is not easy to imagine that they believed it themselves. Their God-Man sails majestically through the upper air, serenely insulated from the politics of his day, apparently behaving with all the subtlety of a low-grade mental defective.

Granted: by the time the Gospels were written the Jewish revolt against Rome had ended, or in the case of Mark, was about to end. Granted: the Gospels were not concerned with by-gone Jewish politics but with presenting Jesus as the saviour of the world. But this leaves a vital question hanging in the air. We know what Jesus meant for the time the Gospels were written, but what did he mean for his own time? Where did he stand on the most pressing issue of his day, which also happens to be the most pressing issue of your day – is it right to fight and possibly kill for freedom?

The Jesus of the Gospels flits as though through a garden swopping repartee about worship, theology and personal morality. In fact, he lived at the heart of a battleground, across which a running war was fought for much of his life-time. Is it not odd, if the Gospels are to be believed, that he was asked to pronounce on such rarefied issues as the heavenly marital state of a much married woman, but no one apparently asked him the more obvious and practical question whether the Zealots were justified in creating havoc by their violent sorties against the Romans?

The Gospel portrait of Jesus is comparable to a biography of a German churchman of the 1930s which makes no mention of his attitude towards the Nazis. One must conclude either that a whole dimension of his life has been suppressed, or else that the vicious politics of his day really didn't impinge upon him to any extent, in which case he was a nonentity. If Jesus was oblivious of all the violence around him, or regarded it as unimportant, then our efforts to make him relevant to the life of our time are futile because he was irrelevant to his own time. And what is more, he was a dangerous, blundering fool, doing ambiguous acts and saying provocative things that invited bloody retaliation upon his followers, all the while protesting that he was being misunderstood.

You don't have to go as far as accepting that Jesus was God; make the more modest assumption that he wasn't a fool, and it is clear that the Gospels cannot be telling the whole story. We can only try to uncover the pieces that are missing by supplying the hidden dimension and interpreting what the Gospels *do* tell us within the context of the politics of Jesus' time.

Josephus versus the Gospels

I am no biblical scholar. All I can bring to bear on this vital issue is some degree of political instinct, experience of another people's freedom struggle against an imperial overlord, and one somewhat biased authority – Josephus.

Of all the books in my library which touch upon the theme of Revolution I little thought that a flaking, leather bound 1849 edition of the *Works of Josephus*, picked up in a Manchester second-hand bookshop, would drive me to a personal reinterpretation of Jesus and his attitude towards the revolutions of our time.

Flavius Josephus was a quisling, a Jew and a Pharisee who went over to the Roman side and became a sort of adviser on Jewish affairs to Titus, the son of the Roman Emperor. In his later days he became a Roman citizen, lived on a State pension, and devoted his time to writing. About the time Luke was compiling his Gospel, Josephus published his account of the Jewish wars against the Romans, and a decade or so later his history of the Jews from the Creation to the end of the Jewish war – *The Antiquities of the Jews*. He was an eye-witness of much of the Jewish struggle for freedom, and though he makes no secret of his Roman sympathies he strikes the reader as neither a coward nor a sycophant. He obviously thought that Jewish resistance to Rome was wrong-headed and wasteful of life and property.

The moral of his story of the Jews during Jesus' lifetime was a simple one. Disaster overtook the Jewish nation at the fall of Jerusalem in A.D. 70 because of the disruptive activities of the Sicarii or Zealots – Jewish freedom fighters who would not see reason and live in peace under a benevolent Roman rule, but with dogged tenacity fought a series of set battles and harassing guerrilla operations to drive the Romans out of the Holy Land. Even when Josephus is castigating the Zealots, his reluctant admiration for them shines through his flatulent prose. They had inherited the fiery tradition that stemmed from Joshua to Judas Maccabaeus, a fanatical patriotism which had kept the spirit of Jewry alive even when their bodies languished under the heel of Assyria, Babylon, Persia, and Greece.

The Zealots, concedes Josephus, 'had an invincible love of liberty for they held God to be their only Lord and Master' – a sentiment Jesus must have echoed from the bottom of his heart. The opening round of their long struggle coincided with the setting of Luke's account of the Nativity – the decree from Caesar Augustus that a census of the Jewish people should be undertaken by Quirinius for tax purposes. In Luke's Gospel this movement of the people to their cities of origin explains why Jesus was born in Bethlehem. 'All the world went to be taxed,' says Luke. Not all of them. Many Jews refused to submit to the census and a bloody struggle against the Romans took place, led by Judas Gamala who, according to Josephus, 'maintained that this census would lead to nothing less than complete slavery and called upon the people to vindicate their liberty'.

So behind the Nativity scene, with its adoring shepherds and browsing sheep, there passes unnoticed in the Gospels a bloody battle that marked the beginning of the Zealots' proud but hopeless struggle for freedom. From this time on, writes Josephus, 'the whole nation grew mad with distemper', adding that there were no less than ten thousand violent disorders in Judea. And Galilee, though not directly under Roman rule, was a most virulent hot-bed of Zealot activity. Its inhabitants, commented Josephus, 'were inured to warfare from infancy'. Both Judas of Gamala and John of Giscala, who in A.D. 66 led the final, fatal revolt which resulted in the sacking of Jerusalem, were Galileans.

'O Sabbath rest by Galilee, O calm of hills above,' rhapsodizes the hymn-writer. In fact, Galilee was electric with defiance, the repository of secret caches of arms, the scene of plotting and strife. Her 'calm' hills were the refuge of guerrilla fighters hiding from the Romans. Jesus grew to manhood in an atmosphere vibrant with militancy, and must have been educated as much on the legends of Galilean freedom fighters as in the Jewish Law. Bloodshed and strife were not a mere memory but a possible daily occurrence. It was in these same Galilean hills, reports Josephus, that the Romans ran to earth a Zealot family, an old man, his wife and seven children. His wife and children begged him to allow them to surrender, 'but he stood in the cave's mouth and slew that child that went out, till he had destroyed them every one, and after that he slew his wife, and cast their dead bodies down the precipice and himself after them, and so underwent death rather than slavery.' This was the other Galilee, a Galilee the Gospels hardly mention.

The Cross was a badge of Zealot defiance long before it became a Christian symbol. Hundreds of freedom fighters died by crucifixion. When Jesus warned that those who followed him must be prepared to take up their crosses, his hearers would understand him to mean not spiritual self-denial but a strictly political fate. They must have assumed that he was embarking on that collision course with the Roman authorities that Zealots had walked in hundreds.

Zealot resistance lasted for the whole of Jesus' lifetime and beyond to the final apocalyptic scene in the desert fortress at Masada in A.D. 73 when the surviving remnants under Eleazar committed mass suicide rather than submit to the Roman Emperor. And Josephus records the Zealot leader's final words, 'Long since we determined neither to serve the Romans nor any other save God . . . for as we were the first to revolt, so we are the last in arms against them. . . .'

It is beyond belief that Jesus was unaffected by this Zealot tradition which held fanatically both to the right to be free and the liberty to worship the only true God. And there is a curious fact which believers in a pacifist Christ do not find easy to explain. Amongst the Jewish people there were four main attitudes to Rome, represented by the Sadducees who were open collaborators, the Pharisees who hated the Romans but were awaiting supernatural vindication, the Herodians, supporters of the puppet-king of Galilee, and the Zealots who were prepared to fight and die for freedom. According to the Gospels, Jesus condemned the Sadducees, Pharisees and Herodians on a number of occasions, sometimes collectively, occasionally separately. But nowhere in any of the Gospels is he on record as having condemned the Zealots. Their methods of resistance were not a minor, episodic theme in the history of Jesus' time; they were setting the nation alight. If their violence was abhorrent he would certainly have said so openly, and surely at least one Gospel would have reported his judgement about an issue on which his opinion must frequently have been sought. It *is* a matter of Gospel record that he chose at least one Zealot to be a member of his inner circle, named Simon the Canaanite by Mark, but identified openly as Simon the Zealot by Luke, who was writing after the dust had settled and the Zealot rebellion had passed into history.

So Jesus spent his life within a highly charged situation in which religion and politics were so interwoven that to utter, as he did, the First Commandment – Thou shalt worship the Lord thy God and him only shalt thou serve – was an act of sedition as well as a declaration of faith. Under such conditions of confusion and violence it is impossible to imagine Jesus living as the Gospels claim, in total isolation from the political struggle and concentrating upon the timeless issues of spiritual religion.

Guilty or Not Guilty?

Drape Josephus's fiery backdrop behind the almost placid account of Jesus' life offered by Mark and a number of incongruities stand out in raw relief. Begin with the crux of the issue, the trial of Jesus for sedition. However the biblical scholar may view Mark's story, from the standpoint of political verisimilitude it is highly improbable. Mark is almost agonized in his concern to show that Jesus was a political innocent who at no time was involved in seditious activities against the Romans; that the Jewish authorities rigged the whole thing and tricked the Romans into doing their dirty work for them. As the Yanks would say, the fall guy was Pontius Pilate who is drawn as a decent but weak sort of character, personally convinced of Jesus' innocence but trapped into executing him when his ploy of offering to release a prisoner to the people back-fired.

The pulpit Pilate, like the Gospel Pilate, is a hand-wringing vacillator in whose character decency and callowness are at war. But this is not how the men of his time saw him. According to Philo, the Hellenistic Jew, Pilate was a tough, mean administrator who did not baulk at using force ruthlessly as the occasion demanded. Philo accuses him of mass murder, outrage, rapine, and pitiless savagery. Far from being a ditherer, Pilate was constantly in hot water with his superiors in Rome for taking the law into his own hands and needlessly stirring up Jewish antagonism. He caused a riot, for example, when he raided the Temple treasury and used the money which was *corban* – given to God – to pay for a new water system in Jerusalem. He was finally fired from his post for using troops to disperse a peaceful religious gathering of Samaritans. Recalled to Rome, he vanishes from history.

By all accounts then, Pontius Pilate was a nasty piece of work with vast experience of waging war against Jewish freedom fighters and matching wits against the Jewish authorities. It is a fair assumption that he would not be easily tricked by the high priests into doing their dirty work for them. He had enough on his plate without becoming embroiled in a domestic Jewish religious squabble. If Jesus was the political innocent Mark claims, Pilate was tough enough to send the Jewish authorities packing. By the same token, if he tried and condemned Jesus, it is a reasonable possibility that either he thought the charge of sedition had some substance or at least that Jesus was a politically dangerous character, better put out of the way.

Then there is the curious episode of Barabbas. To demonstrate that Pilate was more than prepared to give Jesus a fair chance of escaping death, Mark has him invoking the custom, of dubious historicity, whereby a prisoner was released at Passover time as an act of clemency. Barabbas, according to the Gospels, was in gaol as a freedom fighter who had committed murder. Pilate, says Mark, hoped that the people whould choose to free Jesus rather than Barabbas. But Pilate would have been a raving madman to give such a dangerous character as Barabbas an even chance of freedom. Colonial overlords do not go around releasing deadly opponents at the height of a bloody freedom struggle in deference to a religious observance they don't believe in.

And if Jesus really was as insulated from the freedom struggle as Mark claims, it would be a fantastic misjudgement on Pilate's part to assume that the people would ask for his release rather than that of a rabid nationalist. The obvious parallel, though needless to say without any character-reference, is the people of Zambia at the height of the freedom struggle being given the choice of setting free either Kenneth Kaunda or the Archbishop of Central Africa. The good Archbishop would be the first to admit that he would have been a poor second to a nationalist leader in a popularity poll. I, for one, cannot credit that Pilate would give the people a choice between Barabbas and Jesus, and *assume* that they would choose Jesus. If the procurator had seriously desired to free Jesus by such a device, he would obviously have matched him against a much weaker candidate for popular acclaim. He could have hauled some minor felon out of his well-filled gaol, so that the contrast in stature would have made the people's choice a foregone conclusion. To put up an itinerant preacher, who, we are told, kept clear of politics, against a national hero was a gaffe no colonial administrator of Pilate's experience could possibly have made, since no one knew better than he the strength of Jewish nationalistic sentiment.

So we come to Pilate's final attempt to get Jesus released – his pathetic plea to the crowd, 'What, then, shall I do with Jesus called the Christ?' This suggests an abdication of responsibility that does not tally with Philo's estimate of Pilate. He had the power, the authority, and the experience to execute Jesus or free him at will, without passing the buck. And here it is the crowd's psychology that defies explanation. Jesus, after all, was a Jew, and no people in the history of the world have shown such fantastic national solidarity. Jesus was a Jew, at the mercy of a worshipper of heathen Gods, a blasphemer and Jew-killer. In their eyes, the most miserable wretch who crawled the gutters of Jerusalem was one of the Chosen People, God's Elect. Yet in a final twist to the drama that defies logic they howled for Jesus' death. Pilate is vindicated as having done his best, the blame for the killing of Jesus is laid squarely upon the Jews, both authorities and common people.

Because Mark's account of the trial is so improbable, this does not in itself mean that Jesus was guilty of sedition. But a tremendous amount hung on the fact of his innocence in early Christian propaganda. By the time Mark was writing his Gospel the life of Jesus had already gathered to it all kinds of theological overtones. Mark's opening verse, 'The Beginning of the Gospel of Jesus Christ, *the Son of God*' indicates that Jesus was believed to be Divine, and Paul, whose thought dominated the Church (except in Jerusalem) had interpreted his death as the key to a scheme of universal salvation whose nub was that the supremely innocent one had died sacrificially for the utterly guilty. So there was considerable theological pressure on the writers of the Gospels to show that Jesus had been unjustly condemned and executed. Even had Jesus been rightly convicted as a rebel against Rome, this would not necessarily strike a mortal blow against the doctrine of his atoning work, but it would certainly have blurred the neat edges of the salvation scheme by introducing all kinds of political issues.

It is still arguable that Pilate was right in putting Jesus to death for insurrection. Luke, writing when the Jewish War had passed into history, details the charges against Jesus in a way that makes his trial more explicable – stirring up the people, refusing to pay tribute, and claiming political messiahship. Luke obviously thought these accusations fantastic, but there is little doubt that had Pilate the slightest suspicion about Jesus' involvement in such acts he would have executed him out of hand.

If, instead of accepting as a foregone conclusion that Jesus was innocent of the charge of sedition, the Gospels are studied from an attitude of agnosticism, Jesus does and says a number of things which were ambiguous, given the inflammatory situation Josephus describes.

Pay Up and Smile?

Take the issue of the tribute money. According to Mark, the Pharisees and Herodians try to trap Jesus into declaring his position on the most explosive issue of the day – 'Is it right to pay tribute to Caesar or not? Should we pay or should we not?' The Zealot position was absolute. According to Josephus they would not even touch a coin with Caesar's superscription on it, let alone put a cent into Roman coffers. If Jesus said that it was right for the Jews to pay tribute he would lose his popular following – if, on the other hand, he said it was wrong, he had given clear evidence of sedition. His answer, 'Give to Caesar the things that are Caesar's and to God the things that are God's' is taken by Mark to show that he was not guilty of sedition; the Jews could pay tribute without being disloyal to God. This epigram has become the corner-stone of a theological doctrine of the State which grants it legitimate sovereignty in its own sphere. Wrote Lord Acton, 'These words gave the State, under the protection of conscience, a sacredness it had never enjoyed and bounds it had never acknowledged.'

I doubt it. One has only to ask: what, in the eyes of a devout Jew, legitimately belonged to Caesar in the Holy Land? The answer is – nothing. The Romans had invaded the land of a free people, they ruled by no other sanction than force, and extracted tribute as a form of brigandage. Throughout their long history, the Jews had never wavered in their belief that everything that touched them, their land, its people, and its wealth, belonged to God. If God had his due, Caesar would get nothing. So if Mark is reporting a genuine saying of Jesus, the form of his answer might be ambiguous, but its meaning, given the mood of the people, was clearly seditious. It is as though members of the Underground in Occupied Europe had asked a patriot whose judgement they respected whether they ought to help the Nazis ransack their country of its treasures, and had received the reply, 'Give the Nazis what is coming to them!' A passing *gauleiter*, unfamiliar with the idiom, might find such an answer unexceptionable, but the questioners would recognize fighting talk when they heard it.

Jesus' answer seems to me to be fighting talk, and not a clever evasion of the issue. If Jesus was being deliberately obscure, or if he meant something quite different from the interpretation ordinary people might put upon his words, we are back to the point that he would have been a blundering fool of the kind who shouts 'Fire!' in a crowded cinema and after the resulting stampede protests that he was merely clearing his throat. The tribute issue was not a theological school talking point. The lives and liberty of Jews depended upon their attitude towards it. It would be criminally irresponsible of Jesus to confuse the people in order to make a nice debating point against the Pharisees and Herodians. I do not believe that Jesus was a fool, and I do believe that on this issue he would both weigh his words with great care and also take full responsibility for the counsel he gave.

Two other points strengthen this view, one trivial, the other important. There is this tiny detail in Mark's story – in order to make his point, Jesus has to send someone away to fetch a coin. He was carrying no money. This could be sheer accident, but it is just possible that he shared the Zealot conviction that it was disloyal to God to touch or handle coinage issued by the Romans and bearing a heathen superscription. The more important point is that the people were obviously satisfied with his answer. They gave him a rousing welcome when he entered Jerusalem, and openly talked of him as Messiah. They may have misunderstood the nature of Jesus' mission, but never for a second would they countenance a collaborator with Rome as God's chosen leader. Therefore, they must have interpreted the answer of Jesus to the Pharisees and Herodians as a resounding 'No!'

Jesus Shows his Hand

In challenging the idea of a pacifist Christ, what are we to make of the Triumphal Entry into Jerusalem, or, more important, what were the people present at the time to make of it? Jesus borrows an ass, thus acting out an Old Testament messianic prophecy, and solemnly rides over the Mount of Olives into Jerusalem. The ride becomes a triumphant procession. The people demonstrate their support and many openly acclaim him as Messiah, whilst the priests and Pharisees look on, helplessly bemoaning his popularity. The pattern of events makes it plain that this was a carefully planned operation and not a casual entry which blossomed into a spontaneous demonstration. After entering the Holy City, Jesus makes his way to the Temple, then leaves again to spend the night at Bethany. It was a ceremonial journey, loaded with symbolism.

Christian preachers make much of the point that Jesus' own concept of messiahship and that of the masses of the Jewish people were widely divergent; those Festival crowds come under heavy fire in Holy Week Services for failing to see what Jesus was getting at. But the point at issue is not what Jesus thought he was doing, but whether the crowds had any justification for believing that he was doing something else. I think they had, and must conclude either that Jesus was making a responsible bid for the leadership of the Jewish nation or that he was inciting the crowds to violence by a high-minded lack of sensitivity to their mood and reasonable expectations.

However exalted the idea of messiahship set out in the Old Testament at its most profound, for over a hundred years the Jewish people had been schooled to expect a Messiah whose role had strongly political aspects. He was to be a liberator who would drive out the Roman invader and restore Israel's lost glory. Works such as the *Psalms of Solomon*, *The Assumption of Moses*, and the *Second Book of Enoch*, all written in the recent past, had nourished the flickering hopes of the Jews of Jesus' time that help was on the way to strike off their chains and shatter the Roman Eagle. And who can blame a subjugated people for seeing deliverance primarily in terms of freedom rather than some more elevated view of salvation?

Jesus must have known the political connotations placed by ordinary Jews on the role of the Messiah, yet he chose to ride into Jerusalem solemnly acting out that role at a time when the mood of the people was at its most militant and fervent and then, we are told, expected them to see the Suffering Servant through the garb of a political liberator. It takes some crediting. Again the question must be posed – was he a fool? If not, he would surely have avoided raising false hopes by sparking off a demonstration that was bound to misfire and possibly lead, through patriotic fervour, to a bloody confrontation with Roman forces. *That* crowd in *that* place at *that* time must inevitably have thought he was making a play for power. And indeed, whether as Suffering Servant or political liberator, he was still challenging Roman authority for the allegiance of the Jewish people. Either Jesus was naïve beyond belief, or else he had laid the ground for some kind of political as well as spiritual coup, a fact the early Church may have seen fit to suppress because it did not jell with the concept of the pacifist Christ and universal saviour they were at pains to portray.

And if the Triumphal Entry were not enough to convict Jesus of politically ambiguous behaviour, he proceeded to cleanse the Temple, an act which Christian apologetic has proclaimed as a blow against the commercialism of religion and profanity in the most sacred of all places. In fact, Jewish scholars have claimed that the money-changing operation in the Temple, far from being a monstrous system of graft, was an absolute necessity at a time when money was notoriously unregulated and in a place where experts were needed to change the multifarious coinage carried by pilgrims from many lands into the comparatively reliable and standardized Tyrian currency. The selling of sacrificial animals, too, at controlled prices, prevented the growth of rackets outside the Temple precincts.

The nub of the charge against the Temple commercial operations was not that they were corrupt, though this is very possible, but that the system was carried on by the High Priest and his cohorts under licence from the Roman authorities. The Temple had become the haunt of Roman collaborators and it was a standing outrage to patriots that the sacred heart of their faith had been polluted by so-called Jews who not only acknowledged the sovereignty of the Roman Emperor but also made daily sacrifices in his honour.

Jesus' action must have been seen by the people as a blow struck for the integrity of the Jewish people as well as a vindication of the righteousness of God. Who could blame either the Romans or the Festival crowds for reading into the Cleansing of the Temple a symbolic condemnation of any collaboration with the Romans? For every loyal Jew, freedom or servitude began at the Temple, and it is interesting that when the Zealots made their final, fatal bid for freedom in A.D. 66, their first act was to repeat what Jesus had done and occupy the Temple, ejecting the quisling High Priest and his officials. To spiritualize Jesus' attack upon the Temple system into a plea for the purity and holiness of true religion is to ignore completely both the political significance of the complex of operations centred on the Temple and the strength of the people's feelings about them.

It is difficult to imagine the numerous Temple officials standing around and allowing Jesus unaided to overturn the moneytables and drive out the animals. He could easily have been overpowered unless he was accompanied by some of the crowd who had enthusiastically welcomed him into Jerusalem. It is even more difficult to believe that 'the insurrection in the city' which Mark mentions, but does not describe, had nothing to do with the succession of inflammatory actions Jesus performed when he made his bid to assume leadership of the Jewish people. Whether that bid is seen in political or spiritual terms, the end result was the same – trouble for the Romans and their Jewish puppets and a firing of the hopes of the people that freedom was at hand. Jesus was either a responsible leader of a freedom struggle which had both political and religious implications, or else he was playing with fire and inviting others to get burned.

Finally, there are those strange references in the closing stages of the Gospel drama to the carrying and use of weapons. Jesus' famous saying, 'I came not to bring peace but a sword . . .' is easily explained away by its context, which shuts out any possibility that he was talking literally: 'For I have come to set a man against his father, and a daughter against her mother. . . .' The image of the sword is obviously a picturesque way of describing the division and hostility that he was bound to cause. The reference in Luke to the incident at the Last Supper when Jesus advises his disciples to sell their coats and buy swords is more difficult, but it could be argued that he was again speaking elliptically of growing hostility likely to reach the proportions of open violence. A statement such as 'Facing what you are facing, you could do with a couple of swords each!' need not be taken as a literal command. It might be a rueful comment on the general situation.

But . . . there is the incident in the Garden where a disciple cuts off the ear of a member of the High Priest's retinue. Jesus' rebuke and warning, 'Those who live by the sword will perish by it!' well suits the image of the pacifist Christ. Yet the question is posed: why were the disciples armed at all? The fact that Jesus forbids them to fight their way out of the trap does not dispose of the issue. That could have been a tactical rather than a moral decision. For a pacifist leader to allow his inner circle of followers to walk around armed comes near to making a mockery of his teaching. Gandhi would not permit a weapon in his sight, let alone allow his closest disciples to be armed. The Gospels unflaggingly portray a leader who would countenance only suffering love as the instrument of his will, yet apparently those whom he is grooming to carry on his work tramp around with swords clanking at their heels. The picture conjured up is as incongruous as that of a team of Quakers setting out on one of their missions of reconciliation with rifles slung over their shoulders. It is very odd.

Given the confused situation of all freedom struggles and the rough-hewn justice that is often meted out, I cannot see that Pontius Pilate was wrong, in the interests of Rome, to put Jesus of Nazareth to death. Even accepting the story of Jesus' actions set out in Gospels concerned to prove him innocent of sedition, he was at the very least a threat to peace and good order. Those who, either through naïvety or design, incite others in a time of rebellion must expect short shift from trigger-happy imperialist governments. That is what Jesus did, and what he got.

'Jesus and the Zealots'

I had struggled this far with inadequate scholarship to a position where it seemed that the orthodox view of the pacifist Christ was open to question when there fell into my hands Professor S. G. F. Brandon's book, *Jesus and the Zealots.** This was a full year after its publication in Britain. What comment and reaction it had provoked I had no way of knowing – Central Africa is hardly the theological cross-roads of the world. But on the issues to which I could apply little more than political instinct, Professor Brandon brought to bear massive and wide-ranging scholarship. His work is not only a more audacious challenge to religious orthodoxy than all the outpourings of the new theology; it is the standard text for any Christian trying to make theological sense

*S. G. F. Brandon. *Jesus and the Zealots*. Manchester Univ. 1967.

of the revolutions of our time, even though the Professor does not stray by so much as a page out of the world of Jesus' time.

His argument cannot be compressed without perverting it, so closely reasoned and detailed it is, but in outline his view is that Mark's Gospel, as the first written account of the career and death of Jesus, put across an interpretation which the other Gospel writers, with odd variations, followed. Because Mark was writing from Rome at the time the Jewish War was reaching its climax, he had some tough explaining to do, particularly about the Roman execution of Jesus for sedition. The lives of the Christian community in Rome could well have depended upon his skill in showing that the execution of Jesus was a tragic mistake. He lays the blame on the Jewish authorities who plot Jesus' downfall, and explains how a reluctant Pilate is, by a sad mischance, persuaded to have him killed. Jesus was never disloyal to Rome. As his answer on the tribute money issue shows, he advised the Jews to pay up and smile.

So an explanation of Jesus' death designed to meet the needs of Roman Christians in A.D. 71 became the orthodox view of the Church and was reinforced by the demands of theology – Jesus was the incarnate Son of God who, being sinless, died to save the world. And because this was his mission, he insulated himself from the domestic political issues of the day.

After examining in great detail such incidents as the Cleansing of the Temple and the Triumphal Entry into Jerusalem from the viewpoint of an historian rather than a politician, Professor Brandon concludes that Jesus was at least in basic sympathy with the Zealots, but that his political vision had an additional dimension provided by the conviction that he was the Messiah. Whereas the Zealots made the Romans the chief target of their terrorist activities, Jesus challenged the Jewish quisling supporters of Rome and made a bid for political leadership of the people at the Triumphal Entry into Jerusalem which was also a carefully planned claim to messiahship. His bid failed and Jesus died, crucified not between two thieves but between two Zealot freedom fighters.

Though the concept of the pacifist Christ prevailed in the early Church, one account of Jesus' life which might have challenged it perished in the obliteration of the Jerusalem Christian Community in A.D. 70. This Church, under the leadership of Jesus' brother, James, was intensely nationalistic, and shared many of the concerns of the Zealots, as well as believing that the crucified Messiah would return to claim his Kingdom and vindicate Israel. These Jewish Christians gave Paul a rough passage for apparently taking lightly the special spiritual status of Israel in his concern to preach a universal Christ who seemed to bear little resemblance to the Jesus they had known.

So you have the judgement of an eminent Christian scholar that Jesus anticipated you as a freedom fighter by two thousand years, and suffered a fate that you might well be called upon to share.

CHAPTER SEVEN

LOVE AND VIOLENCE

My summary of Professor Brandon's book is a travesty of his powerful argument, but it is provocative enough to raise some obvious and difficult questions. How Professor Brandon would deal with them I have no way of knowing, and must not commit him to my answers. Being prepared to believe that Jesus was involved in seditious activity against Rome, I must battle as best I can with the implications of that assumption.

No Perfect Politicians

The first concerns the sinlessness, or moral perfection, of Jesus. There is much more at stake here than his technical innocence of the charge of sedition. When the Church sings, 'He died to atone for sins not his own', the supposed injustice of his condemnation is regarded as the final irony of a blameless life which has given birth to the theological and devotional image of the Lamb led to the slaughter. But if Jesus were involved in the freedom struggle against Rome, this whole dimension of the Church's preaching and theology is undermined, for he was operating in an area of life, that of extremist politics, where one's only practical choice is often between the bad and the worse, with no infallible way of telling them apart. Shabby compromises, nasty but necessary actions, desperate decisions, are the daily commerce of a resistance movement. A sinless paragon could not enter that seething turmoil or even understand the motives of those he found there, let alone share them. A great man might, in such conditions, preserve his integrity, but never his purity.

With this problem I have no great difficulty because nothing material in my faith depends upon Jesus having been sinless in the most literal sense. And I doubt that many modern theologians would nail down the issue so uncompromisingly as Oswald Sanders, who writes, 'In their pages, the Evangelists present the portrait of a Man, a real Man who displays absolute perfection at every stage of development in every circumstance and relationship of life.' Those who take this line find themselves performing verbal gymnastics and heroic feats of reconstruction to explain away Gospel incidents which appear to show a less than perfect Jesus – harsh, scathing, sarcastic, and impatient. Nor is it easy to see how a sinless man could genuinely immerse himself in life – whose nature is tentative, limited, riddled with paradox – and still emerge recognizably human.

Jesus himself was a greater realist about the ambiguities of history than those who seek to protect his unique virtue. In his parable of the Wheat and the Tares, he rejects the possibility of perfection in this life and warns that the best actions of which man is capable let loose a flood of consequences, both good and evil, upon the world. Our experience confirms his pessimistic conclusion. Human virtues are twisted out of shape by a warped Creation – spirituality shades into remoteness, probity hardens into legalism, earnestness tends towards aggression, fervour escalates into fanaticism. The liberal grow lax; the firm, bigotted; the convinced, self-assertive. To argue that Jesus was exempt from this bias in the texture of life either through his miraculous birth or by special decree from God is to destroy his manhood and turn him into a Greek deity who walked the earth bending its laws to suit his whim.

A sinless man would be a monster, a shapeless blur, lacking *individuality* which results, surely, from the balance struck between our strengths and weaknesses? This is why Tom is not Dick or Harry, and Jesus was not Peter or Judas. Personality is moulded by a thousand responses to life for which we pay in character development. Even our victories and defeats are relative, because only in fairly tales are humans faced with absolute moral choices. So when the hymnwriter sings, 'In all things like thy brethren thou wast made, except free from sin', shorn of its indifferent poetry, his statement is strictly nonsense. A sinless Jesus would be nothing like his brethren, for however humble his demeanour, he would by-pass history instead of experiencing it.

What others see as the sinlessness of Jesus, I would describe as a quality of integrity, a single-minded determination to do, in concrete situations, what he believed to be the will of God: that, plus two other things – an unparalleled openness to his fellow human beings in compassion, and the wisdom to detect what is of ultimate significance in the immediacy of issues. And I see no reason why he ought not to have believed that it was God's will for him in first-century Palestine to help release Israel from a heathen yoke. We talk of the God of History, by which we mean presumably that his will, far from expressing itself in vague generalities, is often shockingly specific. We boast that in the Old Testament God used a Persian king, Cyrus, to destroy the power of Babylon and restore the Jews to their own land. Why should we baulk at the possibility in the New Testament that God willed his obedient servant to lead the struggle to free Israel from Roman domination? I am not suggesting that this was the totality of God's will for Jesus, but it could have been an element in it. Nor am I claiming that the significance of Jesus' death can be fully exhausted in political terms. But would it be an unworthy end for the Messiah to die for Israel's right to worship the one true God?

Love and Violence

The second problem is more formidable. If we reject the idea of a pacifist Christ, must we come to terms with a warlike one? And if so, how can this militancy be reconciled with his teaching, whose recurrent theme is the law of love as the supreme standard of human life?

A casual reading of the parables of Jesus rules out of court any suggestion that he was a dewy-eyed sentimentalist who carolled about love because the harsher side of life was a closed book to him. He drew many of his illustrations from the areas of society where men contend for power and speak the language of violence. In one place he talked about a king who orders those who will not accept his rule to be put to death; somewhere else, about another king who, in anger, razed a city to the ground. He used the images of robbers binding strong men and attacking travellers, crooked agents, tough businessmen, domineering slave-owners. This raw streak in his teaching makes nonsense of Renan's description of his 'sweet and idyllic nature'. He was no lotus-eater, shutting his eyes and mind to the tough, lurid and unpleasant aspects of life. And this sharpens the dilemma. Knowing the way of the world, he still said that we should love our enemies, turn the other cheek when provoked, and forgive with monotonous regularity.

This issue has got to be faced head-on. The love-ethic of Jesus is absolute. He does not even offer the loop-hole that the strategy of love is a kind of higher wisdom which is bound to pay off sooner or later. And its motivation seems to be entirely religious – we ought to forgive because God forgives us; we should love indiscriminately because that is the way the grace of God operates. We cannot pin any political label on Jesus, but a society based upon his literal teaching would be anarchistic – perfect love would remove the need for the compulsions of law, the checks upon power, the adjudications of justice. And where love is perfect all distinctions between what is our own and what is someone else's would disappear. As Reinhold Niebuhr has written, 'The social ideal of Jesus is as perfect and as impossible of attainment as his personal ideal.'

I am writing about politics, and must stick to my terms of reference, but it must be frankly stated that politics was not the prime concern of Jesus. He put first the quality of the personal lives of his followers. The first bastion of the Kingdom of God is raised in the human heart, and it is there the work of regeneration begins. Neither you nor I would be a Christian if we did not believe this to be the kernel of the Gospel.

Yet if Jesus was a man at all, he was, like every man, a political being, living within social structures protected from chaos by the use of power. Those who say that Jesus kept aloof from domestic political issues in loyalty to a higher destiny must recognize that by so doing he was making a political decision with terrifying implications. Politics is about power; how it is used and to what end. If a man decides, for whatever reasons, that he will not touch power, he is abdicating to others the right to decide how it will be used. This is a political judgement, and he cannot evade some share of the responsibility if unscrupulous men use that power destructively.

There is a dilemma here on which all Christians are impaled, and Jesus the man could not side-step it. The love-ethic which Jesus commands us to make the law of our being is not only impossible of fulfilment in history but, if pressed to the limit, becomes self-defeating. It can, of course, be retorted that the love-ethic only seems impossible because no nation or political party has had the courage to try it. G. K. Chesterton is often quoted to the effect that Christianity has not been tried and found wanting, but has been found hard and not tried. This is the argument of many pacifists, and it is a shaky one. They expect institutions such as the State or political parties, which can neither give nor receive love, to operate according to the laws of love which govern the purest relations between persons.

Even those who hold strictly orthodox views about Jesus, and interpret him according to the traditional schemes of theology, cannot resolve the paradox that the heart of their Faith, the Cross, is at one and the same time the vindication of the love-ethic and yet proof positive that this ethic is beyond fulfilment in history.

Take, for example, the classical theory of the Atonement which says a struggle took place between the crucified Christ and the legions of Hell. According to the theologians, the powers of evil, though defeated in principle, still operate to extend the area of chaos in the human heart and throughout society. And it is all too clear in concrete situations that the only barrier against the onset of chaos is the use of a degree of constructive power, involving compulsion, which the pure love-ethic must rule out of court.

Or there is the simpler view of the Cross as the supreme example of the redemptive power of sacrifice. Love, we are taught, can only be fully realized at the expense of life itself. Obviously, an individual can choose the way of the Cross, but no larger grouping such as a nation or a political party ever has done or ever could do. For the way of sacrifice must be freely chosen. No one can enjoin it upon others or choose it for them without destroying the basis of the ethic. One could go further in rejecting the simple transposition of the way of the Cross into a political philosophy by showing that the State exists for purposes which are the precise opposite of the way of love unto death. Its role is to preserve life, to shield its members from extinction, whether by threat of outside enemies, internal chaos, or natural hazard. That is what the State is for, and politics serves to strengthen and clarify these objects. To attempt to impose the love-ethic upon the State through politics is to invite it to deny the law of its being.

The truth is that the love-ethic in its pure form cannot come to terms with the compulsion which is a necessary feature of all organized life. And it obscures political problems when it causes men to seek an ideal possibility in situations which offer only a number of realistic alternatives, none perfect, few satisfactory, all morally relative. The love-ethic followed through to its limit will deny the Christian any participation in political life at all because he will seek in vain for a political system pure enough to deserve his devotion.

Unless we are to retire to the mountain top and pray our lives away, we must operate within society as responsible men, which means making decisions on behalf of others – in industry, through the ballot box, even within the family circle. We are entitled to follow the love-ethic in sacrificing our own interests without hope of reward, but we cannot justify the sacrifice of interests other than our own. We cannot compel those for whom we are responsible to choose sacrifice. So, willingly or unwillingly, we must follow the hard law of collective relations and settle for the only kind of justice society has ever known, that which results from harmonizing legitimate conflicts of interests, if necessary by the use of superior power.

So whether or not Jesus was involved in the freedom struggle against Rome, unless he was commanding his followers to contract right out of society, he burdened them with an unresolvable dilemma by the absolutism of his moral teaching. I prefer to believe that he not only posed this dilemma for others but also shared it himself by accepting the limitations which the gravitational pull of history exerts upon pure goodness in the realm of politics. This does not mean that he was a murderous thug. The merciful soldier is not an uncommon figure in history. Maybe this is the quality which the centurion who saluted Jesus sensed in him. And our century has canonized its own brand of saint, the resistance fighter who is poetic or philosophical by nature and of towering stature. The book, *Dying We Live*, edited by Helmut Gollwitzer,* contains the letters of no less than fifty-six German Christians executed by the Nazis for crimes which ranged from attempting to assassinate Hitler to inciting the German people to rise and purge themselves of Fascist pollution. Each one proudly declares that he did what he had to do out of loyalty to Christ. Who doubts that Jesus approved their actions? Possibly he did more – and walked the same road.

May there not be evidence that he felt the full agony

*Fontana, Collins, 1958.

of the love-ethic dilemma in his doomful sayings about the destruction of the Jewish nation?

> And when he drew near and saw the city he wept over it saying, 'Would that even today you knew the things that make for peace! But now they are hid from your eyes. For the days will come upon you, when your enemies will cast up a bank upon you and surround you, and hem you in on every side, and dash you to the ground, you and your children within you, and they will not leave one stone upon another....'

This tragic outlook on his nation's future may reveal the anguish of someone being torn apart by the knowledge that what he is doing is inevitable and yet ultimately self-defeating, in contrast to the vainglory of the unreflective militants who believed that Valhalla lay just beyond the next battlefield.

Or again, traditional faith sees the agony in the Garden, the bloody sweat, the inner turmoil, as the humanity of Jesus warring against acceptance of the way of sacrifice. But self-sacrifice, however painful, is a purely loving act. Maybe it was the other way round; that his anguish was due to the necessity of choosing a road that was morally compromising. Maybe he sweated drops of blood, not at the thought of suffering pain himself, but of causing pain to others. That is a much more fearsome thing. Yet possible, because even single-minded obedience to the will of God must, within history, involve opening up new possibilities of evil as well as extending the rule of goodness.

It is the law of love which shows up the partiality of all human insights and the ambiguity of all human actions. Who would feel this more acutely than the one who taught that law, and lived it out as no other man ever has? The love-ethic is not merely irrelevant to politics. If it were, we could brush it aside and pigeon-hole our lives, being idealists in our personal relations and realists in our public policies. But love stands as a judgement over all our historical activities, reminding us that the limits of the possible have been set, not by God's edict, but by the totality of man's sinfulness.

If Jesus were truly a man, and not a visiting deity from another planet, he must have chafed at the limits of the possible, but there is no evidence that he made the mistake of believing that any actions, even his own, could cut a swathe of perfection through historical chaos. He never taught that the Kingdom of God, where love holds undisputed sway, is the final outcome of any earthly strategies, the ultimate move in some infinitely complex chess game. The New Heaven and the New Earth are not shapes wrought out of the flawed material of history, but gifts of God from Beyond. The Kingdom of God is not something which happens *in* history but something that happens *to* history. And the choosing of the time when the texture of history is changed, Jesus taught, is solely God's prerogative – 'No man, not even the Son of Man, knows the time. . . .' His ignorance of this eschatological moment put Jesus firmly where we also stand – choosing from amongst imperfect alternatives the courses of action which are effectual signs of that Kingdom.

All this seems to me to be implied in believing that Jesus was a man. And it is to Jesus' manhood that we must tenaciously cling: what is called his divinity can take care of itself. Faith in the man may lead us to believe that he was something more, but if there is any doubt about his true manhood, then no matter how strongly we believe in his divinity he is cut off from us by a chasm that cannot be bridged, and Christianity takes its place amongst the mythical religions. Furthermore, history is empty of saving power.

Political Messiahship

Many Christians are repelled by the thought of a political Jesus. This has a lot to do with the nature of politics and the reputation of politicians. They are happy to believe Jesus might have been a carpenter, a craft which, before the advent of the trade unions, had the ring of honest toil about it. Or he could have been a peasant, a station in life which has got certain romantic overtones – the smell of the good earth and all that. But a politician!

They have a point. Politics in the ancient world, and especially in the desert lands where the tradition still persists, was both a dirty game and a deadly one. Power changed hands by means of the bludgeon rather than the ballot box. Politics and violence were synonymous. A tough man or family dynasty ruled until poisoned, hacked to pieces, or otherwise relegated to their due place – the cemetery. Retiring politicians didn't get the chance to deliver their seals of office to the Queen; their severed heads were stuck in some prominent place to announce that their jobs were vacant. Every political campaign was a freedom struggle. Those who were tired of being pushed around did some pushing on their own account.

There were places where they organized things in a less messy fashion. When politicians seek a respectable pedigree, they rhapsodize about the Greeks gravely dropping their plaques into stone jars and Roman senators debating laws which, though arbitrary if you were not of the right class, were still majestic and strong. But no sensitive politician would wish to claim descent from the Jews who, by all accounts in the Old Testament and elsewhere, were a bellicose, quarrelsome people whose religious genius was matched by their capacity for intrigue.

Now, say the orthodox, can you really see Jesus doing that sort of thing? And the honest answer is, No, I can't. But then there are all kinds of things he must have done which I can't imagine him doing because I am a twentieth-century bourgeois parson and not a first-century Semite. In spite of the well-founded warnings of wise men that it is not possible to get at the historical Jesus who stands behind the Church's faith, the attempt must be made. It won't do to accept what the learned Doctors of the Church have said Jesus was up to. Every man must decide for himself what Jesus thought he was doing.

The Church's Jesus is a gleaming diamond of a man. So he should be. Two thousand years of polishing have gone into smoothing out his rough edges. Two thousand years, that is, less the three centuries or so bishops and theologians spent quarrelling in a contest presided over, so we are told, by the Holy Spirit, to decide just who Jesus was. The ordinary Christian of that time could not have been orthodox if his life had depended upon it because there was no consensus on doctrine. Nevertheless, for a very long time the Jesus-Industry had a monopoly of the best brains, so it is not surprising that every awkward question you can ask about the Man from Nazareth has a balanced doctrinal answer. You may not believe it, but you must give credit for ingenuity.

This Herculean labour of love paid off. Every period in Church history had its own Jesus who looked at home there and answered just the questions men of the day were asking. It isn't the least bit odd then, that Jesus also fits our time like a glove. But it *is* suspicious, because he oughtn't to. The more completely he merges into our landscape, and the better he speaks our language and enters into our thought-ways, the deeper ought to be our fear that this Jesus originated not in a backwater of the Roman Empire but in the recesses of our own minds.

Every missionary knows how hard it is to get inside the heads of the people of another culture. No psychiatrist is likely to underestimate the problem of getting inside the head of a patient even if he happens to be the man next door. So a Doctorate in Divinity seems an inadequate reward for tracing the workings of the mind of a first century Semite, who is cut off from us by a succession of civilizations, the rise of modern science, the Industrial Revolution, and the Space Age. Yet we claim to be able to do it: our efforts at psycho-analysing Jesus pour from our pulpits and off the religious presses in a ceaseless flow. Schweitzer saw the danger clearer than most when he warned, 'The historical Jesus will be to our time a stranger and enigma. . . . He passes by our time and returns to his own.'

This universal Christ, with the chameleon-like gift for adapting himself to every place and epoch, makes things too easy for us. Any man can find in him not only his heart's desire but also a judicious blend of all the virtues he hopes to see vindicated in his own time. Our ideas about Jesus tell us more about ourselves than they do about him. I search the Gospels for a freedom fighter and Jesus strides out, sword in hand; the pacifist looks there for the great advocate of non-violence and is rewarded by a glimpse of the triumph of suffering love. As George Pfister wrote, 'Tell me what you find in your

Bible and I will tell you what sort of a man you are!'

If it is Jesus' motives we are after, the most important question is how he saw his role as Messiah. The Church teaches that Jesus took his cue from the Old Testament picture of the Suffering Servant. We find this line of thought reassuring for three reasons: it suits the character of Jesus as he is described in the Gospels; it shores up our doctrines about his atoning work; and it appeals to us as sensitive men sickened by the cruelty, mass violence, and aggression of our time. So Jesus, to order, acts out a ritualized behaviour pattern which satisfies the demands of our theology. It is all very convenient, and a little unreal.

In human terms, Jesus was a first-century Jewish prophet and not the eighteenth-century creature of Mr Charles Jennens, librettist of Handel's Messiah. No real man's life moves forward to its goal with the precision of a journey undertaken according to instructions given in Bradshaw's railway guide. Self-insight is always tentative, diffuse, and on occasions downright contradictory. Western theology and psychiatry reject such an untidy view of man, and have mounted great campaigns to unravel the knots in his behaviour and set before him clear-cut goals. The result is that those areas of experience where the wild music of life is made are declared out of bounds by great notices warning of the danger of Sin and Insanity.

Pre-scientific peoples make no solemn covenant with Bradshaw to draw into any station at a given time. They wander, back-track, and move pretty much as the raw or balmy winds drive them. Our failure to take this into account when trying to understand Jesus exposes our Western cast of thought. The Western mind is a problem-solving mind. We cannot live with contradictory ideas; we must settle for one or other, or else evolve a third which harmonizes the other two. The non-Western mind can hold contradictory ideas in tension without trying to resolve them. It is also open to experiences which the Western mind rejects as irrational or superstitious. Westerners tackle theology like everything else – as a series of problems to which answers must be found. This may explain why Christianity's main appeal has been to those in the Graeco-Roman tradition, rather than Semitic and Bantu peoples. It is too unremitting in its pitiless logic and too constricting in the experience it allows its adherents.

Had Jesus a mission at all in the sense of a planned campaign carried through doggedly to its bitter-sweet climax on Calvary? What we identify as drive may well have been drift – wanderings slowly steadying into direction; strange ideas gradually solidifying into convictions. Even the Gospel accounts of his travels look more like the perambulations of an Eastern *guru* than the systematic itinerary of a Western executive.

A non-Western Jesus, far from choosing firmly between Isaiah's conception of the Messiah as Suffering Servant and the hopes of ordinary folk which were centred on a political liberator, may have had a whole jumble of ideas in his mind without wanting, or being able, to resolve them into some neat pattern. The raw material of his thinking about what it meant to be Messiah must have been drawn from many sources – politics as well as religion, contemporary writings as well as the Old Testament, the legends of freedom fighters as well as the sermons of the rabbis. His mind would be fed on the strange but potent diet of religious tradition and political radicalism – the tradition was in his blood and revolution crackled in the air. As Kenneth Kaunda has written about the pre-scientific mind, 'The African mind does not find it easy to think in terms of

Either-Or. It is open to influences which make Both-And seem desirable.'* 'Both-And' is the magic key to the history and psychology of the Jews; that blend of love of tradition and revolutionary fervour which has always been their genius and sometimes the cause of their downfall. How could a Jewish Messiah avoid feeling this tension? And if he didn't try to resolve it, he would be driven to do things totally inexplicable to our tidy minds.

Kenneth Kaunda also says that the pre-scientific mind, besides holding contradictory ideas in tension without trying to reconcile them, sees nothing odd in acting upon whichever idea seems to fit the circumstances. Didn't Jesus? And isn't this why an ounce of insight may be worth more than a ton of Western scholarship in trying to explain his more contradictory Gospel sayings? All prophets who live in one particular time and yet speak of truths which stand for all time sometimes behave in a way which some would call inconsistent. The Mahatma Gandhi, for example, was an enigma to many Westerners. Most of the time his goodness was so guileless as to border on the naïve, but occasionally he deployed a serpentine political cunning which shocked his less understanding admirers. Cynics might condemn such unexpected twists of behaviour as expediency. But plain contrariness is also the hall-mark of a genius, whose struggle for self-understanding will never end so long as he draws breath.

Piety and Politics

From the time of the Exodus, when the Jewish people trekked out into the desert in search of nationhood under God, their politics and religion were in such a

**A Humanist in Africa*, Longmans, 1966, p. 30.

glorious muddle that it was only possible to make sense of either when they were united in the persons of great leaders such as Moses. Indeed, the nation always got itself into the most serious trouble when power-loving kings on the one hand or stiff-necked priests on the other tore these two strands apart and set piety and politics in opposition to each other. It was the prophets who got the people of the Exodus on the move again with their twin concerns – spiritual renewal to make the nation worthy to serve the only true God, and political freedom to enable it to do his bidding. Jesus offered a demoralized nation a final chance of renewing its lost glory in his proclamation of the nearness of the Kingdom of God – an image which welded together personal obedience to God and radical political action. The acceptance of the kingly rule of God, so Jesus taught, was primarily a matter of spiritual renewal by way of repentance, but its political overtones were unmistakable. It was a nation in the totality of its life he was calling back to God, rather than isolated individuals; and not just any nation, but one which in its highest moments could not divide its allegiance between God and any Caesar.

When Jesus offered himself as the focus of Jewish unity, and I do not see how else his Triumphal Entry into Jerusalem can be explained except as such an offer, he made a decisive intervention in the freedom struggle. Granted, his role was strategic rather than tactical. There is no evidence that he concerned himself with detailed plotting or active guerrilla operations. But as Messiah he both embodied and proclaimed truths whose outworkings would make continued Roman rule intolerable for an already restive people. In distinguishing between the strategic and tactical aspects of the freedom struggle, I am not trying to have my cake and eat it by suggesting that Jesus was to some extent politically involved but stopped short of staining his hands with blood. There is no such thing as innocence in extremist politics; only varying degrees of guilt. To invite the people to follow him was to set them on a collision course with the Roman authorities. He was putting in train a series of events the consequences of which were unpredictable. The over-zealous in their patriotic fervour were likely to take his messianic claim as a signal to intensify their terrorist activities.

Yet the profundity of his teaching, with its emphasis on compassion for the little people of the earth who are always the worst victims of armed clashes and civil disorder, would make his attitude to the freedom struggle more complex than that of the Zealots. He was too reflective to believe that there was a simple political solution to Israel's plight. Whether the ordinary people would appreciate the subtlety of his position is another matter. He did not live long enough after the Triumphal Entry to find out.

To locate Jesus so directly in the political issues of his time does not, in my view, undermine whatever is meant by his incarnation, but strengthens it. The Jesus of the pietists was never truly incarnate because he was apparently able to pick and choose the areas of life he would enter, and carefully kept out of those which might compromise him. Politics is man's most representative activity because it imposes order upon all his other concerns and puts his values to the test of practicality. We put our faith to the test of practicality when we try to serve Jesus at the pressure-points of society. It would be devastating to our morale if Jesus never put his own teaching to the same test of practicality.

This is not the whole story. I believe what is called the divinity of Christ is another way of saying that God acted uniquely through, and gave universal significance to, an historical life. God rewarded the unparalleled obedience and unequalled love of Jesus by establishing him as the pattern of the new humanity. And God both endorsed that decision and put it into effect by raising Jesus from the dead.

For some reason the Resurrection is the Christian doctrine with which I have least difficulty. That sentence of graffiti written on the walls of an American university, 'There'll be no Easter this year – We've found the body!' doesn't cause me a tremor. Nor do the contradictory or inconsistent details in the Easter Gospel. The mechanics of the Resurrection are fascinating in a morbid kind of way, especially for devotees of the occult, but they are of no importance. We are way out of the realm of historical proof at this point. Belief in the Resurrection, like all acts of faith, is a stab in the dark which thousands would say pays off, and I am amongst them.

I believe God vindicated the obedience of Jesus by bringing him back into history, though not in bodily form, to gather together a New Israel, recruited from all the nations of mankind, which would get on with the business of renewing the earth from the point where the Old Israel went astray.

To go any deeper into this theme is to start writing a different book. Let's summarize the story of Jesus by saying that God may have chosen a more political instrument for his revelation and man's redemption than most Christians want to believe and others dare to hope.

CHAPTER EIGHT

SALVATION BY VIOLENCE?

So Jesus was young, coloured, and poor, and I believe he took part in Israel's freedom struggle in obedience to God's will. He said nothing to suggest that political freedom was an end in itself. To keep the First Commandment, '. . . and him only shalt thou serve!' he had to strike against a false God imposed by force upon an unwilling people. I am not trying to reinterpret the whole of Jesus' life and mission in narrowly political terms; merely claiming that a strategy of rebellion was one of the things which obedience demanded and he did not shrink from it. Certainly, mercy and suffering were key themes of his life, but neither of these qualities necessarily outlaws revolution. Mercy may *require* revolution – the use of violence to destroy a system of greater violence which prevents millions from being free men before God. And revolution is sometimes the only situation in which suffering can have any positive, creative significance, instead of that passive, self-purifying character which enables non-resisting men of strength to save their own souls but leaves the souls of the weak in jeopardy.

If it's New, it's Good!

I am not really offering *Salvation by Violence!* as the rallying cry of a new Reformation, though on second thoughts there is a kind of truth in that slogan. When Moses asks God what his name is, he gets the cryptic reply, 'Call me "I will do what I will do" ', which is presumably God's picturesque way of warning the Hebrew leader that he can only be known in history by his actions. Man knows that God is around because things change. And it is the speed at which God is changing things, coming up against man's resistance to change, that makes violence inevitable. When water freezes in the pipes, nothing short of a blow torch will get torpid water molecules zipping around again. The torch sears and molecules collide, but that is the price of movement. When life gets bogged down, God provides the fuel for the torch the revolutionary wields. God must have change or he cannot *be* in any sense that can be humanly understood, and if violence is the only way he can get change, he will not baulk at it – if the Old Testament is any guide.

We are always being told to get back to God. But there *is* no way back to God: we can only fight our way forward to him. Far from being a Rock of Ages, majestically immobile as the storm rages around, God changes within history at a rate that makes us dizzy. That slogan of the cheaper sort of advertising – 'If It's New, It's Good!' – may be demonstrably untrue when referring to new mystery ingredients in old detergents, or new bits of chrome on last year's model car, but there is a more profound level of life where it makes sense. *Anything* which introduces a new factor into a deadlocked situation is good, even if at first sight it appears destructive. But it must be *new*, not just different; no reshuffling of old packs, no novelty for its own sake. Paul Tillich, preaching on God's word to Isaiah – 'Behold, I am doing a new thing' – declares: 'The new is not created out of the old, not even out of the best of the old, but out of the *death* of the old.'*

The world of the *Unyoung*, *Uncoloured*, and *Unpoor*, for all its technical innovation and physical speed, is a static world because no new human possibilities can break out from its inner deadness. In this sense it is a Godless world. In resisting whatever will catalyse necessary change, it is fighting against God and so is ripe for destruction. Hence, *Salvation by Violence!* may not be so far wide of the mark. God is the inspiration of every strategy which breaks down the old to make way for the new. He is behind *all* the revolutions of our time. Not every one of them is achieved by violence, but many are.

The Church versus Revolution

To expect the Church to come to terms with such a rigorous truth is to cry for the moon. To my knowledge, the Church as represented by her hierarchies, assemblies and professional saints has never supported a revolution. It is an odd thing that the Church is able to rest without too much discomfort at the heart of the most elaborate system of violence the world has known – Western society – and yet cries to high God about the evils of violence if some desperate peasant tries to hit back at the juggernaut which is crushing him. After the U.S. Strategic Air Command, the Church's Jesus is the world's most effective peace-keeper – for keeping things, that is, the way we want them.

The Church's abhorrence of revolution cannot be explained simply by saying that she shares the general corruption of the West, though that is true. Indeed, in contrast to the rock-hard complacency of her society, the Church at least has the grace to feel uneasy about

* *The Shaking of the Foundations*, Penguin, 1962, p. 182.

the deformed shape of the world and show contrition for her share of the responsibility.

The problem is much deeper. Revolution would rob the Church of the thing she values most – not her wealth, property, and privilege, but her sense of continuity with the past. She boasts of being the guardian of the faith once delivered to the saints, and in her rituals re-enacts events of two thousand years ago. She derives comfort from the things which don't change: 'Change and decay in all around I see, O thou who changest not, abide with me', or 'We wither and perish – but naught changeth thee' – a somewhat bleak assurance, I always feel. Her frantic hold on the past is seen at its most absurd in that doctrine of the Apostolic Succession according to which the authority of bishops depends upon their having been tapped on the head by someone who was tapped on the head by someone who was tapped on the head by St Peter – a plain case of elevating Evolution over Resurrection and trusting in dead ancestors instead of a living Christ.

It is not difficult to identify the true enemies of revolution within the Church. Popes, Cardinals, and Archbishops with their princely trappings, traditional privileges, and antique charm are no more bulwarks against revolution than were the be-wigged aristocrats of Louis' court on the eve of the storming of the Bastille. They are living proof of the need for revolution. Nor is Fundamentalism, with its over-heated Gospel of individual salvation that would vapourize you more effectively than a laser beam, an anti-revolutionary force. Literal interpretation of the apocalyptical bits of the Bible may even prepare conservative Christians to expect cataclysm, although they draw all the wrong conclusions from it. The real enemies of revolution in the Church are the reformists, the new theologians who are trying to get a new accommodation between the Christian faith and a society which needs to be swept away. If they are successful, they will provide a Christian rationale for the continuance of the West, and to that extent hold back the future. It would be quite unjust to allege that such radicals are not concerned for the plight of the world's depressed millions; far from it, they are well represented in the protest marches and picket lines. But their basic aim is to ensure the survival of the Church, and to help Christians to hang on to their faith in a time of revolution. These are honourable motives, but largely irrelevant to the task of getting justice for mankind.

As the tempo of change accelerates, we must expect theologies of revolution to burst out all over the Church. Yet nothing we in the West have to say about revolution has much value, because we have more to lose than gain from it. Deep down in our gut, at a level lower than our consciences, we like things the way they are. It is as hard for a Westerner to face up squarely to the prospect of revolution as for a patient to amputate his own leg – he finds it terribly difficult to cut deep enough or let sufficient blood. Any theologian writing about revolution on a full belly and from a position of privilege will instinctively try to hang on to much that ought to be dispensed with. He is talking about revolution but thinking in terms of reform. A really honest Western theology of revolution would probably be apocalyptical rather than politically radical – preparing men for life in the catacombs. For just as nineteenth-century pagans received the Gospel in awed silence as a power from another world, so we in the West will sooner or later be the dumb recipients of a terrible truth from outside which cannot be fitted into our traditional schemes of thought.

For this reason, I am afraid that left-wing Christian thinkers, anxious to demonstrate the relevance of their faith in a turbulent time, are wasting their energy in trying to express Christianity as a revolutionary ideology. This is not because their ideas are wrong, but because they are thinking in terms of an ideology at all. They want to structure revolution; to impose a system upon it which will cease to be scaffolding and become a strait-jacket. Most of the men who make revolution in our day will do so not because they have convictions about God, man, society, or anything else, but out of a terrible anger and a deadly despair.

The moral is plain. Herbert Butterfield, in his *Christianity and History*, advises his readers, 'to hold to Christ, and for the rest be totally uncommitted'. In practice this is impossible. You cannot have the Person without the System, Christ without Christianity. You can claim that Jesus is at work throughout society, or that his spirit is operative in men and movements totally divorced from the Church. But the Christian, in any moral sense of that term, is anti-revolutionary because he is committed to a system which will try to impose order upon revolution and, if successful, destroy it. Whether, on the other side of revolution, we might catch a glimpse of a Jesus who is not trapped in the system, we have no way of knowing, though the Resurrection as the transcending of an historical dead-end gives us hope that this should be so. But in the meantime we are faced with a straight choice, and it is an intolerable one. Only a strong man can let go his hold on every institutional manifestation of Jesus in the confidence that Jesus will not let go of him. This is precisely what the Christian who contemplates revolution will have to do. I don't think it was a coincidence that Bonhoeffer's search for 'religionless Christianity' came to a head when he was in prison awaiting death for a revolutionary act. For a short while he had entered a world to which his theology was not only irrelevant but a handicap; where a man might have to reverse the drift of a whole life-time and do the unthinkable – hate rather than love for Jesus' sake. I think it was Tertullian who said that one of the greatest sources of happiness in heaven would be the spectacle of Roman emperors roasting in hell. One of the themes of a down-to-earth theology of revolution might be the role of healthy hate in nerving men to do what any normal understanding of love could never allow. But it will take a theologian with a strong stomach to write that sort of thing.

Unstructured Revolution

Even if the Church is against you, I'm sure that Jesus is not against you. How could he be? The present system makes it impossible for millions to love their neighbour. Those in deadly competition for a crust of bread, or burning with resentment that their children starve whilst others flourish, know no law but that of the jungle. Even ordinary human affection withers in the fiery blast of perpetual conflict. Writing of the condition of poor families in Mexico City, Oscar Lewis, quoted by Harvey Cox, comments:

> The most striking things about these families are their general malaise, the rarity of happiness or contentment, the rarity of affection . . . above all, where hunger and discomfort rule, there is little spare energy for the gentler, warmer, less utilitarian emotions. . . . *

**On Not Leaving it to the Snake*, S.C.M. Press, 1968, p. 106.

Love is between people. How can the hungry love the well-fed, or blacks love whites when they are thrown together in a system which treats the one as more than a person and the other as less? Love, compassion, and forgiveness have no place in the animal world, and that is where the majority of mankind lives.

Jesus said that the truth makes us free. By the same token, there are some truths which only free men can appreciate. The children of Israel had to be free before they could reject other gods and pledge themselves to Jehovah. Only free men can enter the Kingdom of God. This freedom is not exclusively political, but that element is central in our day. It is not systems of philosophy or theology which destroy a man's humanity and drive him into a corner where he has neither freedom of thought nor freedom of action. Political systems do that. So do economic laws and social patterns. The little people of the earth who are trapped, as the Spaniards say, between the sword and the wall, may not be far from the Kingdom of Heaven, but the required effort is beyond them. And those who preach Justification at them – that it is God's grace rather than their own efforts which saves them – have little idea of the spiritual demoralisation and utter despair that numb the responses of those who hang on to life by a thread. God has done nothing else for them, why should he save them, and even if he does, what has changed?

Those who through cynicism or fear discount modern revolutions because they are unstructured – carried out without any master-plan – are deluding themselves. We are living in the time of the death of all systems. Revolution begins as a blind thrust for freedom, not as a crusade to change the world. A man suffocating to death in an airless cellar does not plan the rest of his life before kicking down the door. This is why the dialogue between Marxists and Christians, begun in the 1950s, to which radicals pin such hope, is largely an academic exercise. It is an operation to mate two discouraged systems on the off-chance of giving birth to a third which will save the world, or at least our own skins. The radical fervour of each soon hardens into a new orthodoxy. Since the summer of 1966, China has been tearing herself apart as the architect of the original revolution, Mao Tse Tung, thrashes around trying to break out of the system he has imposed on his country. In less than two decades, the revolutionary flow has iced over and solidified. And Regis Debray, now languishing in a Bolivian prison, has commented that Castro's success in carrying through the Cuban revolution was due in part to his failure to read beforehand the writings of the classical theorists of revolution. He was free to act entirely as the needs of the moment dictated.

The students who first occupy university buildings and then settle down to debate their next move, are not, as their detractors sneer, *ersatz* revolutionaries because they have no master-plan. This is the shape of revolution in our time – begin by smashing down the barricades and then see what the terrain looks like on the other side. So imprisoning or killing left-wing intellectuals in the belief that they direct the mob will not hold off the reckoning. Revolutions are no longer made by bearded scholars writing their major works in the Reading Room of the British Museum. Indeed, there is a widespread contempt for intellectuals on the other side of the barricades. Writes Debray:

> Castro once blamed certain failures of the guerrillas on a purely intellectual attitude to war. The reason is understandable: aside from his physical weakness,

> the intellectual will try to grasp the present through preconceived constructs and live it through books. He will be less able than others to invent, improvise, make do with available resources. . . . *

This is another reason for distrusting theologies of revolution. They try to relate the 'new thing' God is doing to what he has done before. They stem from that Western thirst for explanation which is prone to locate God in the ultimate *Why* of things instead of the immediate *How* of them. Christians claim to be the People of the Exodus with no settled abode on earth, but they have a horror of uncontrolled change and shy away from the concept of perpetual revolution – one upheaval succeeding another as a new tyranny replaces the old and must in turn be dislodged. In such a time of confusion, there is no *Why* of things that the human mind can fathom. So if God is not in the *How* of things, he is strictly irrelevant.

Every revolution requires what Regis Debray has called the freeing of the present from the past because the past contains no redemptive element, no untapped possibilities. Only the death of the past offers mankind a new chance. For this reason, the Messianic role of preaching the Gospel to the poor and releasing captives belongs in our day not to the Princes of the Church, many of whom are mere tinkerers with society, nor even any longer to Marx and Lenin and Mao, but to those who are making revolution *at this moment*. Ten years from now, their revolution will probably have degenerated into a new oppression, but for the time being, large sectors of mankind are given hope. Martin Luther once warned:

* *Revolution Within the Revolution?*, Penguin, 1968, p. 21.

> God's grace is as a passing storm of rain which does not return where once it has been: it came to the Jews, but it passed over; now they have nothing. Paul brought it to the Greeks, but it passed over; the Romans and Latins had it, now they have nothing. You must not think you have it forever.

'You must not think you have it forever' . . . what is true of God's grace applies equally to the spirit of revolution. Indeed, doesn't the one embody the other? Revolution is evanescent, short-lived. You Rhodesian freedom fighters may overthrow the settler regime and usher in a new era, but the day will come when others will have to get rid of you because your rigid grip is throttling to death that to which you have given birth.

So the prophetic mantle of Jesus passes to Marx, Lenin, and Mao, and then on to Castro, Ho Chi Minh, and Torres. But none is entitled to wear it for long. Each has his time of creativity and inspiration, and millions are rescued from oppression and hunger as a result. Such times pass; success destroys the revolution and the struggle must begin again. The law that both good and evil consequences flow from all human actions leads us to expect such a pattern of events. Yesterday's prophets of mankind become its enemies tomorrow. But such men in their time deserve to be called prophets because they have challenged the belief derived from the Greek element in our civilization that history is predetermined. They have taken their stand as the Hebrew prophets did, and as Jesus did, for an open future which will be what men make it.

Unstructured revolution can only succeed where a society is ripe for dissolution. Otherwise overwhelming fire-power, modest reform, or judicious bribery will nullify it. Fidel Castro did not overthrow the Baptista regime by superior tactics or majority support. He gave a sharp push and the system collapsed under the weight of accumulated corruption. This is why the West has cause for fear. Student revolt, Black Power, Latin American guerrillas are, in themselves, a derisory challenge unless . . . unless the rottenness of the West's foundations will no longer bear the weight of material affluence soured by spiritual arrogance. Then one day, like a forest giant eaten out by ants, it will collapse if a child leans against it.

'It Can't Happen Here!'

It might be justly claimed that my expansive talk about world revolution is a far cry from the specific issue which concerns you; that it is idiotic to see revolution in the West foreshadowed in the firing of a handful of shots for freedom in the Zambesi Valley. I admit the truth of such criticism and would only reply that I am not such an incurable romantic as to think of revolution as the immediate prospect of world-wide upheaval or even total national disruption in the West. It isn't possible to be revolutionary all the time and everywhere at once. The immediate goal is more modest – persistent intervention at the pressure points of society, not in the first place to destroy the power of the *Unyoung*, *Uncoloured*, and *Unpoor*, but to erode away their self-confidence, the arrogant assumption that the world is organized for their exclusive benefit.

Any action, however limited, which threatens the institutions of the West with the aim of sweeping them away rather than reforming them, is truly revolutionary. But to get this far, the radical has to smash down a barrier in his own mind and recognize that Western society has exhausted its capacity for change – it is at an evolutionary dead-end. The tactics of the reformer and the revolutionary may be identical. It is their loyalties which are different. The revolutionary no longer has any sentimental attachment to the traditions and way of life of the West. He takes no pride in its achievements, nor is he mesmerized by its power. He is dedicated to smashing that power in the name of all humanity which has become his family, nation, and race. No narrower loyalty makes sense to him.

The ferment in Latin America, Africa, and Asia is already undermining the West's ability to make other people miserable by imposing its will upon them. Millions of mice are nibbling away at the extremities of a moth-eaten lion. For British radicals, the Rhodesia freedom struggle is crucial. The by-play between the British and Rhodesia Governments underlines the determination of the *Unyoung*, *Uncoloured*, and *Unpoor* to preserve for as long as possible the privilege and supremacy of their own kind in Southern Africa. Rhodesia is a microcosm of the nature of the world struggle. Those proposals for a constitutional settlement of the Rhodesia rebellion which issued from H.M.S. *Fearless* were more than a device for off-loading an acutely embarrassing political problem. They symbolized Britain's irremediable preoccupation with the past. Mr Smith's government did not sail away from the *Fearless* bearing in its hands an officially-blessed independence only because it was too dim to see that it had won. The safeguards on which Mr Wilson insisted and at which Mr Smith baulked would have been totally unenforceable for the same reason the rebellion was not crushed in the first instance – Britain's abhorrence of using force against her own kinsfolk. Black Rhodesians must now take matters in their own hands, not merely to win their freedom but also to repudiate once and for all the right of the *Unyoung*, *Uncoloured*, and *Unpoor* to haggle amongst themselves over the lives of the rest of mankind in a more sophisticated version of the old slave market. Only when Black Rhodesians, and White ones of good intention, snatch their country out of the West's grasp will she realize that the old game is up.

You do not need to be told you are in for a tough time, yet you and your revolutionary brethren of the Third World are the envy of thousands of young people, and some not so young, in the West. Your revolution is under way. But what about Western radicals who feel anger and disgust at the antics of the powerful Troika who rule their world, and yet don't know what to do about it? In many ways, they are living their revolution through you. It is a genuine expression of Christian love to accept an unconditional commitment to justice and freedom for others. But what about their own revolution? Yours cannot now be halted; theirs cannot get started.

Most of your fellow-travellers in the West have reluctantly rejected any prospect of the renewal of their society through existing political structures. There was a day when Britons of spirit and idealism might look to a socialist party to spear-head the struggle for world brotherhood, and by so doing to release new power into its own society. But radical anger at the Labour Government's cynical squandering of generations of sacrifice has passed by way of contempt into a numb realization that the space occupied by socialism in British society covers a gaping hole through which one looks down into nothingness.

The signs of doom hang over Britain. The collapse of parliamentary democracy and the deep contempt felt for politicians; ferment in institutions such as trade unions, universities, and Churches; social dislocation at every point from football crowd violence to the growth of racial intolerance; permanent economic crisis which is symptomatic of something more fundamental than badly misjudged fiscal policies – all tell the same story. Things are coming apart from the centre outwards.

There are those who take comfort in believing that revolution is out of the question in Britain. They forget it has happened before. According to Pitirim Sorokim, the land of political sobriety suffered no less than one hundred and sixty-two major or minor revolutionary clashes between A.D. 656 and A.D. 1921, from the Great Rebellion at one end of the scale to an insurrection of the Wessex Yeomanry in A.D. 725 at the other. It was one of Britain's prophets of national complacency, the Earl of Strafford, who in 1638 wrote, 'The people are in a great quietness and if I be not mistaken, well satisfied with His Majesty's Gracious Government and Protection'. Four years later, England was being torn apart by civil war.

The affluent West likes to think that only countries whose population is sunk deep in poverty and oppression are ripe for revolution. Hence, say the apostles of a totally unfounded optimism, Britain's prosperity is an insurmountable barrier to revolution. As One Man One Vote has been the rallying cry of colonized peoples seeking self-determination, so One Family One Car is seen in the West as the best guarantee of political stability. This is a dangerous assumption. As Crane Brinton has pointed out in his *Anatomy of Revolution*, the four classical revolutions of the West all occurred in countries which were economically progressive. Stuart England, in the years of personal rule before the Long

Parliament, had more widely diffused wealth than ever before in her history. Nor was there any grinding poverty in the New England of the Stamp Act. In France revolution was made possible by the refusal of the prosperous middle classes, lawyers, bankers, civil servants, and farmers, to go to the aid of a government which got into deepening trouble throughout the 1780s. And even though Russia suffered a complete breakdown of government in 1917 as a result of her defeat in the First World War, she had, in the first decade of the twentieth century, taken great strides towards economic maturity in the Western style. Material prosperity is not a safeguard against revolution. The divisiveness of greed sometimes succeeds in shattering the unity of the State where the bare-footed peasantry fails.

Britain is already bobbing around like a cork in the wake of an ocean liner as the tidal wave set up by the outward explosion of the depressed two-thirds of the world threatens to engulf her. Soon even the most complacent sectors of her society will be unable to see their nation's relationship to a world in revolution in terms of knocking sixpence off every half-crown's worth of overseas aid. They will have to choose between the past and the future for survival's sake. And Britain's only future lies with the poor world. She cannot afford to match the stakes the U.S. puts down to stay in the imperialist game. The dispatch of a handful of bobbies to Anguilla stretched her purse; a Vietnam is totally beyond her. And the West will have to finance bigger and better Vietnam-style operations if she hopes to stay on top in those parts of the world where she has no business to be anyway. Britain's Moment of Truth cannot be long delayed. Then all kinds of forces will come into play whose nature and direction it is impossible to predict at the present moment.

Extremism as a Way of Life

If there is one thing sillier than discounting the possibility of revolution in the West, it is to idealize it. Those who choose to walk through fire must count the cost. Extremism is an appallingly narrow way of life. I am not just thinking of the sacrifice of good food, bright lights, and a warm bed for the heat and stench of the jungle, but of the irreversible change which takes place in the character of those who reject the sum of human values in favour of one burning obsession. In 1868, the anonymous author of a short pamphlet called *The Revolutionary Catechism* wrote:

> The revolutionary is a dedicated man. He has no interest, no business, no emotions, no attachments, no property, not even a name. In his innermost depths he has broken all ties with the social order. He knows but one science, that of destruction. The tender sentiments of family, friendship, love and gratitude must be subjugated to the single cold passion of the revolutionary cause.*

Desperation is the driving force of extremism, and desperation is the supreme simplifier, reducing all the complexities of life to one sharp, blinding issue and its inevitable resolution. Without warping his character, man cannot make a single good – not even social justice – the central business of living, with everything else relegated to a subordinate place. Unreasonableness is the essential attitude of extremism, for those who see reason cease to be extreme and are lost to the cause. It is the sheer intensity of concentration upon a single dimension of life, or even upon one apocalyptic event, which

*Quoted by Gaucher, *The Terrorists*, Secker & Warburg, 1968, p. 3.

sends brave men to their doom, unable to distinguish between martyrdom and suicide, sacrifice and waste. Man has a great capacity for histrionic gestures. Revolution provides him with a stage, a skeleton plot, and an audience.

Can the Christian do it? Can obedience to Christ be confined within such narrow limits without degenerating into fanaticism? I frankly doubt that the Christian faith *as we have learned it* can accommodate the revolutionary who really means business. But then I don't believe that the Christian faith as we have learned it can open a way into the future, either. The revolutionary is probably the truly tragic figure of our time, risking the loss of salvation that his brethren may be saved and have wholeness of life. Yet it is surely true that the manifold acts of our life have no value unless the total act of living can be justified. And it is necessary for at least one of the things we do in living to have absolute value. The Christian who becomes a revolutionary takes the risk that in a world locked up in the past, the blow which opens the way to the future may count as the 'one thing needful' about which Jesus talked. He steps beyond any traditional understanding of Jesus into a spiritual and ethical No Man's Land in the hope that the future is where God is. We men of reasoned faith tend to forget that we come from blood-thirsty stock. The story of our salvation began when a captive people smashed their way into the future, taking Moses' word for it that they would find God there rather than amongst the tombs and monuments.

Or possibly another image is more appropriate. Maybe the revolutionary reverts to being a pre-Christian and stands where John the Baptist stood. He not only warns of the wrath which is to come, but also embodies it, laying the axe to the root of the tree in